Free the ...

Cynthia Gough

Cynthia Joy Field

New Wine Press

New Wine Press
P O Box 17
Chichester
West Sussex P020 6YB
England

Copyright 1993 © Cynthia Gough

All rights reserved. No part of this publication may be reproduced, stored in a retrieval system, or transmitted in any form or by any means, mechanical, electronic, photocopying or otherwise, without the prior written consent of the publisher.

Short extracts may be used for review purposes.

Scripture quotations are from the NIV, The Holy Bible, New International Version. Copyright © 1973, 1978, International Bible Society, published by Hodder & Stoughton.

ISBN: 1 874367 15 9

Typeset by The Electronic Book Factory Ltd, Fife, Scotland

Printed in England by Clays Ltd, St. Ives plc

Dedication

To my children,
Sally and Stephen.

The Aim

'To touch the hearts of those who love Me, and love My Body the Church, and to reveal to them the pain and hurt which their divisions cause Me. And through the testimony of My guiding hand in your life, to encourage and strengthen their faith.

To reveal the need for spiritual warfare to come against the principalities that have entrenched themselves in My Church, and to encourage believing prayer, using your testimony of My revelation to you of spiritual warfare.

To use My word to confirm the revelations I have given you.'

A 'word' from the Holy Spirit

Acknowledgments

A big thank-you to all those who have encouraged and helped me to write this book. Especially to Janet Mason who looked after me, prayed me through, checked every page, and helped to find the references.

Thanks to Adrian for bringing me God's directive; and to all those in my Church family who believed in this book getting finished and published, when I had doubts.

Thanks to my sister Edwina, for typing the manuscript, providing lunches, tea, and lots of chat over our knitting; I wonder how we ever finished it!

Thanks to Sarah for reading the manuscript and giving helpful comments, also to Paul Kent.

Thank you to Eileen Wallis, who guided me and helped me in the early stages of writing this book, and who was an encouragement and inspiration to me.

Also thank you to the many dear friends who have given me permission to quote them and use their names, (a few have been altered to preserve anonymity.)

We live in exciting times for Christians, and it's going to get even more exciting. Alleluia!

Contents

Introduction

On March 10th 1989 I went to a church celebration which was being held near my home in Totton, Southampton. All the churches in the area had been invited, and, as the speaker was to be Colin Urquhart, many of the members of each church attended.

Colin had already had a dramatic input into my life on an earlier occasion, precipitating me into repentance and baptism, but I wasn't expecting anything particularly life-changing to occur this time.

The large hall was packed, and the Holy Spirit was powerfully present. Colin spoke, giving several words of knowledge. (People had already been released and healed during the worship). Another word of knowledge came: 'There is someone here that God wishes to leave their employment to work fully for Him.' Was God speaking to me? I had sometimes wondered if full-time teaching as a biologist was all I could do for Him. I left the meeting thoughtfully. I would need time to consider what had been said and I wanted definite confirmation.

As head of department in a large Tertiary College my life was rewarding and fulfilling. I was 56 years old, divorced, and living alone. My married daughter was living in Sheffield, and my son was studying for a degree in Exeter. My job not only supported me financially, but was socially and intellectually satisfying.

What would I live on? I could apply for early retirement, but I only had 12 years pensionable service. I knew that if God was asking me to leave my work, I would have to trust Him for the finances.

How would I cope without the satisfaction of my job?

I hate being bored, and I would miss all my friends. I had done as much as I could to witness to my colleagues, and to the students at college, and I knew that God had used me to encourage the young Christians in the Christian Union. Surely I was still needed at college?

Having been trained to teach, what else could God want me to do? I hadn't been a Christian for long, and I wasn't young any more (except at heart!) Well, I was going on holiday to Italy at Easter, so perhaps God would confirm this word to me then.

I felt very unsettled during the two weeks in Naples and Calabria. Colin's words would not go away. I cried out to God,

'Why do you want to take away my job Lord? It's my last bit of earthly security!'

There seemed to be no reply, and I knew I would have to start making enquiries when I returned to college for the summer term. I would see what happened if I sent away for the relevant forms.

My union representative didn't think I had any chance of early retirement with a pension, because I was fit and healthy and doing a good job. I told him that even if I didn't get a pension, I would retire anyway, as God was asking me to!

He was exasperated and said,

'But you'll have nothing to live on!'

'I will sell my house,' I replied. 'If God wants me to retire, He will provide for my needs.' Amazingly, I did get early retirement with a pension and, as soon as I heard, gave in my notice.

At that point I had little idea of my income, but had been offered 3 years enhancement. Also, I discovered that I could buy back the 6 years superannuation that had been drawn out early in my marriage to buy a plot of land. I would have a total of 21 years pensionable service; it should be enough to live on, and even to run a car.

Well, what did God want me to do when I retired? Maybe I could work among sixth formers with Nick

Pollard, who carried out missions in colleges in the Hampshire area. I asked Nick if he would like my help, but, as soon as the words had left my mouth, I knew God was saying,

'No; that's not what I want you to do!'

For the next few weeks I had no idea why I was retiring. Then on July 3rd, a friend from the church (who was a fairly new Christian) visited me. When I opened the door, he stood there looking white-faced and worried; he had come to apologise for being rude to me at church the previous day! Poor chap, he was really upset and I hadn't been a bit bothered by his behaviour, knowing he was under considerable stress. I invited him in, and accepted his apology, assuring him that the matter was already forgiven and forgotten. Then he said,

'Cynthia, I have a message from God for you. He spoke it out loud to me! I am to tell you that God wants you to write a book, and that there will be a publisher.' I was stunned. Me, write a book! I knew Adrian hadn't imagined this message – he was a hard working manager of an estate agent. He had specifically asked God to give him something else to say to me, apart from an apology.

God doesn't often speak out loud to people, at least not to my knowledge. It had to be important. I had no idea what this book was to be about, and decided to have my usual summer holiday and to think about the book in September.

On September 1st, the first day of my retirement, I was driving to Lymington to my old friend Betty's funeral. I was feeling sad, returning after many years to a church I was now separated from.

'What is this book to be about, Lord?' I asked.

He said, 'My divided Church, and all the pain its divisions cause Me.'

But what effect could anything I might write have on such an enormous issue? The Lord reminded me of David and Goliath. All I had was the smooth, rounded pebble

11

of my life, the words would be the sling, and that small pebble would fly out under the Holy Spirit's guidance.

Where would I write this book? My home was on a noisy road, and I constantly had visitors and phone calls. I would need peace and quiet. I talked to my friend Janet Mason, who lived in a beautiful, rambling bungalow, set in a large garden on the edge of the New Forest. She suggested that I use Grandpa's room. He had died in February 1986 and his room was empty except when the family came home. It could be mine for the time it took me to write a book.

I had loved Charles, John Mason's father, and I used to call by for a chat on my way home from college. He was a godly Christian man, and his room had been well prayed in. The room was lovely, with patio doors leading out into the garden. Janet found me a suitable table, even making a cloth for it, which matched the heavy damask curtains.

Early in October 1989 I arrived at John and Janet's house, with my pens, notebooks, files and paper, to start writing. I was terrified at the thought of going into the room, and picking up a pen. Suppose nothing happened? Janet prayed over me, I shut myself into Grandpa's room, and started to write.

1
The Vision

Such a lovely day, still, warm, and hot – September 1st 1989.

How can I get in touch with my son, Stephen? There was no reply on the car phone, so I left a message at the office.

I was going to an old and beautiful church set on a hill among fields and woods on the edge of the New Forest to sing for Betty's funeral. Would Stephen be able to come too?

It was seven years since I stood by Betty in the choir, seven years since donning the long purple gown and white collar and cuffs. Should I sing alto or soprano?

Stephen was once chief chorister; now, at 25, a vocalist in a pop group. Betty had been leader of the choir and chief soprano. Her faithfulness was an example to us all. Nothing stopped her attendance at morning service and evensong, and at every wedding and funeral. If she was ill, she still came, sniffing her smelling salts to revive her. Only the red flush on her cheeks told of the fever. Her white, wavy hair was like a crown, her aquiline nose held high. How we loved to sing the descants, our voices soaring like birds.

'Why, Father, did you call me away from the beauty, the music, the joy and peace of this place, my security for eighteen years?'

'Thank you that Betty is now with You, mercifully freed from her cancer-ridden body, before the chemotherapy could take its toll.'

'Your Church, Father, divided.'

At St. John's I must conform. How would I not raise

my hands in worship? How could I not allow you, dear Holy Spirit, to sing through my voice the songs that constantly come to my lips? How will I stifle the soaring freedom that my spirit now knows? Why, Lord, can I not share my new-found freedom with these dear Christian friends that I love, and who love me?

'Please come back, we need an alto,' they plead. 'Now you have retired you can visit us more often.'

What can I say? 'It is too far from home,' or 'Yes, I will try to come and see you all again.' But my heart says,

'I have come out of the cave, from the shadows of worship, into such colour and light.'

How can I tell those still sitting in a beautiful prison what they are missing, as they cling to their familiar shadows? The prison of following conductor and music, of having the right book, of saying the formal prayers, of sitting or standing to order.

'These people honour me with their lips, but their hearts are far from me.'

(Matthew 15:8)

Where are you, gentle Holy Spirit? Are you sitting outside, longing to be invited in, to lead, to comfort, to release, to heal?

'Holy, Holy, Holy, Lord God Almighty, heaven and earth are full of your glory.'

'Where are You Father? How can Your glory pour it's waves of golden light over Your people? Where are You, Jesus? Here You are neatly classified into the middle class mould, everyone tidy in suits and ties, except Stephen who got the message late.' He sat at the back, in old T-shirt and jeans, where he could enjoy the beauty of the anthems. However he had removed his sweatshirt with 'Why be normal?' emblazoned across the front!

Supposing You came in Jesus, scourged and bleeding, and weeping for the pain and suffering of the world, crying in a loud voice,

14

'Give up all, and follow me!'

Would You be sent out for causing a disturbance?

The path of obedience, the narrow gate; few there be that find it.

'Why can't it be easier, Lord? Yet I know Your heart, Lord, I know Your heart, because You showed me. You showed me who it is who still presses the crown of thorns on Your head, making the blood flow and the tears. It is those of us who should most honour and care for You still giving You most pain.'

In November 1979, as a lecturer in a college, I had volunteered to go on a pastoral care course. We would live simply, cared for by nuns. I knew little about nuns; what would it be like to live with them? I wasn't expecting their joy or the sudden desire to stay with them forever, in order to share their simple lives of prayer and service. We would be able to join them for morning mass before breakfast, so I set my alarm clock to rise early and go to chapel.

Already the nuns were there, sitting together in their long black habits, praying. I sat at the back, looking at the white walls, plain and high, with the pattern of windows set in the top, the simple white altar, the big crucifix – such light and peace. Listening to the nuns' sweet voices singing, I was surprised that the mass was so familiar, similar to the Church of England Communion service that I knew so well. How glad I was to be kneeling there with these godly women, sharing their praises, the priest leading us. Then the peace offered to all – no C. of E. formality or embarrassment here; they gladly walked about embracing each other in love.

'Greet one other with a holy kiss . . .'

(Romans 16:16)

We too, who had joined them, were embraced, eyes meeting in the joy and love of Christ.

We had been told we could not join in sharing the

15

bread. This was only possible for those who belonged to the Roman Catholic Church. There had been a priest previously who had allowed this, but he had been taken away, so that the rules of Rome and the Pope would be obeyed.

The invitation came to go forward to receive the Body of Christ, and the visitors stayed, kneeling at the back, watching. Why did a great grief fill my heart? Why did sadness suddenly overcome me, and a few tears? Perhaps I was tired – the term had been busy, and I hadn't slept so well in a strange bed.

We left the chapel, and the day was filled with talk and discussion. It didn't seem possible to talk to the nuns as they waited on us, graciously and quietly. I looked forward to being with them again in the chapel, and to the sweet chanting, the peace of the simple furnishings – golden wood against white walls.

I had become a 'born again' Christian four months earlier in July '79, this despite 15 years singing in a church choir, and believing I was a Christian. Then everything changed – on that night in July, after attending the baptism of two friends in a local Baptist church. Sitting up in bed, I asked Jesus into my heart, to take over my life. I also asked to be filled with the Holy Spirit.

Since then my life had been renewed, full of such happiness, such wonder, and such awareness of Jesus. I hadn't experienced any sadness in those four months, just a heady and passionate love and joy.

So why, as the nuns went forward again to receive the bread, did this grief and sadness fill me? Why were the tears now spilling down over my cheeks? I hid my head, embarrassed at what was happening. Why was I being so emotional? What was the matter with me? I must be tired.

That night I drove back home; Brockenhurst wasn't very far. I would see how Stephen was managing. He was alone in the house, and I could get a good night's sleep in my own bed. I wouldn't be back in time for mass in the morning, only for the lectures and discussions.

Then it was our last evening at Park Place. I went to bed and read and prayed in the simple little room.

'Lord, is it alright for me to go to mass again?'

Then His voice spoke, through my thoughts.

'Yes, but first ask the priest to let you share the bread.' Oh no, the thought filled me with fear – how could I? The priest only appeared in Chapel – I had no idea where he lived, or how to contact him. He would think I was being awkward. What would he say?

But I had promised to obey God, whatever the cost. I would make a condition,

'Yes Lord, I will ask him, but only if You bring him to me, and he starts to talk to me.' Phew!! I felt sure that would let me out of an unpleasant task. I couldn't see any possibility of meeting the priest on my own anywhere. So I slept happily and peacefully!

We had been asked to clear our rooms before breakfast, so the next morning I rose early, packed my case and went downstairs, to put it in my car before mass. The big front door was locked, but there was a key, and outside were the daily papers and milk waiting on the step. I stood looking at the sunrise. It was breathtaking – the sky a golden pink, the sun just appearing, and a warm glow over the grass, stretching out to the trees silhouetted in the distance. The air was crisp and fresh, and the drifts of dead leaves were brown and still.

I carried my case to the car, placed it inside, and locked the boot. Then I turned round, and there, in front of me, was the priest with his dogs! My heart missed a beat, as I remembered my promise the night before. It had happened, I would have to ask him.

'Good morning,' he said. 'Have you enjoyed your stay?'

'Yes,' I replied, 'It has been lovely to be here, but there's just one thing I would like to do – to be able to share in the mass with the nuns.'

17

'Of course you can,' he said. 'You are very welcome to come along.'

'No, I have been twice already,' I replied, 'but I want to take part with the nuns.'

'Why, yes,' he said, 'we will give you the peace.'

Then a third time I asked, 'Yes, I have received the peace each time, but I am a Christian, I would like to take the bread with you.'

His face changed – a look of shock and anger came across it.

'Oh, no, that isn't allowed; it's against the rules of the Church, the Pope has forbidden it.' I looked at him, tears starting to pour down my cheeks.

'But you are denying Christ to me,' I said. He looked startled, then changed the subject.

'Did you come out of the front door? If so, could you leave it open for me? I don't know why, but the nuns don't unlock it, so I cannot get back that way.'

'Yes,' I said, 'I will leave the door unlocked for you.'

I sensed that the nuns did not like what was happening. They had known the joy of sharing mass with other Christians and this priest was saddening their hearts. No wonder they kept the door locked in the mornings. Still, I had been obedient, though it hadn't worked. At least now I would be able to enjoy the mass, the last time to be with the nuns.

This time I sat as near to them as I could, behind them to the right. The peace was offered, but, as I got to my feet, the tears started pouring down my face. How embarrassing, what should I do? An old man who did the washing up came towards me, his lined, brown face and bright eyes so understanding. He said nothing, but held me in a warm embrace. I felt comforted. I went back to my place. Soon they would be going forward for the bread that I was denied. Again the tears began to flow.

'Jesus, what is happening? I have done what You asked. Why am I weeping?' Then deep sobs started to rack my body. I tried to stifle them. I didn't want to disturb the mass.

'Jesus, why am I crying and sobbing and feeling so unhappy?'

Then, through my tears, a vision appeared. It was the face of Jesus, looking so sad. The tears were pouring down His face, the crown of thorns rammed hard on His brow, and blood trickling down. Suddenly I understood. It wasn't me crying at all, but Jesus inside me, grieving that I could not be united with the nuns, and share in His Body with them. Jesus was grieving that His Body, the Church, was broken and divided.

I stayed kneeling in my place.

'Is this what we are doing to You Jesus? Your divided Church, that should be a glorious crown for You, instead is a crown of thorns, giving You constant pain and grief.'

The chapel was empty, I dried my tears, and got up. How could I go and eat now? I had no appetite any more. Slowly I walked out, and then stopped, noticing a beautiful stained-glass window by the chapel. In it, golden flames of fire soared upwards. I stood looking.

'This must be in honour of You, Holy Spirit,' and as I looked, it was as if God was comforting me, and saying that through the Holy Spirit the Church would change. Our differences would be healed, and the grief we gave to Jesus would one day be transformed to joy.

2

Congregational Upbringing

It was many years later that I stood with a group of Christians on a cold and dark February night worshipping God in a churchyard. We had driven to a nearby town, and during that evening we 'saw' the Holy Spirit working to free the church from an evil power. We were in a spiritual battle, and, in answer to our prayers, knew that a mighty group of angels were bringing down their powerful and enormous swords to destroy a demonic being over the church in that place.

How had God led me in the ten years since my vision, to be standing with a group of Christians, battling together for the church? Why was the evil of Church disunity something I longed to see healed?

Like many people, I was brought up with prejudice, and heard criticism and condemnation of other denominations.

My mother had been brought up in the Congregational Church. My father had been a chorister in the Church of England. I was from a mixed denominational background.

My parents were married in the Church of England, but, when three daughters arrived, mother decided that we should all attend the church that she was brought up in. So every Sunday we walked a mile to the nearest Congregational church, Dad coming too.

Houses and bungalows were built on the field opposite our home, and – horror of horrors – a Roman Catholic church. I wondered at the picture of Sir Thomas Moore, over the door, surrounded by gold mosaic that shone in the sun, and I would watch the people going in and out for weddings and funerals.

But mother was shocked by them. 'They go to confession, then go home and sin all over again – all that bowing and scraping and worshipping the Virgin Mary,' she would say.

I wanted to go inside, and see what was happening – was it really that bad? Holy water did seem a bit odd. How could one lot of water be any different from another? What happened when you put some on? How did they do it?

Overcome by curiosity, one day I persuaded a friend to come with me. We pushed open the big door and crept inside.

We looked around; inside it felt nice, so clean and white and peaceful, all those little wooden carvings round the walls of Jesus carrying the cross. Why did they have so many? I counted them; there were twelve altogether. I didn't like the big cross with Jesus on it. We didn't have anything like that in our church. I couldn't understand why we had to walk such a long way twice on a Sunday, when we could have gone just across the road. It didn't make sense, but mother had to be obeyed, and I didn't go into the church opposite again.

Anyway the Congregational church was lovely, very plain and simple, with no pictures anywhere, but the windows were big, and you could look out at the sky and the trees. There were meeting rooms at the back where we went for tea and biscuits after the service, a room upstairs with a stage for productions, other smaller rooms, and a kitchen. We were like a big family, knowing everyone by name, meeting often for socials, with fun and games. During the week I went to Brownies, and when I was older to play table tennis, and to choir practice. Life revolved around the church.

I became too old for Brownies, and the Girl Guides met in a Church of England. Some of my school friends went there, so I decided to join.

21

We were expected to go to church parade once a month, and it was fun lining up with our flags, and processing into the church – we felt really important. But it was sung Eucharist – how our knees ached! As we didn't go forward to take communion, we seemed to be down on them for hours. It was really boring and uncomfortable.

I realised what Mum must have meant about the Roman Catholics – all that bowing and scraping. What was it all about? It all seemed to be a lot of mumbo jumbo. How could they mean it, saying the same prayers every week, and why didn't everyone sing?

In my church a wonderfully powerful sound poured out from the congregation all round you, but here it was just the choir that sang, apart from a few weak notes here and there from the congregation. I was always glad when it was over.

My Mum had a friend who lived nearly opposite. They often had a cup of tea together and helped each other out when needed. Her friend had these strange family ceremonies with candles on Friday nights, and they ate special sorts of food that we didn't have; they were Jews. But according to Mum, Jews were fine, after all Jesus was a Jew. It was only the other Christian denominations we had to watch out for, though as Dad had been Church of England, she didn't say too much about them.

Does every child in a Christian or church-going family suffer the same confusion and learn the same prejudices? Why was it I could never accept and go along with them, always curious to know the truth, biding my time, till I could find out for myself, believing that our differences didn't really matter, it was Jesus that mattered?

Surely if we all loved Him, we could enjoy being part of any Christian group? Perhaps it came from Dad, who, like me, said nothing, keeping his own counsel. He had foregone the church–going patterns of childhood and youth, to worship wherever Mum wanted to be – it wasn't important to him. He could love and worship God anywhere.

22

But Christmas seemed to be the one time when every-thing was different. Christians were prepared to drop their barriers, and get closer, as we all knelt in awe and wonder before Jesus in the manger. Who could start to have a theological argument in front of a baby?

'. . . unless you change and become like little children, you will never enter the kingdom of heaven.'

(Matthew 18: 3)

Even the soldiers trained to kill the enemy, came out of their trenches, as they heard the sound of 'Stille Nacht,' rising to greet the new born King, and shook hands with each other, exchanging gifts of peace. Tomorrow they would be back again behind their guns, to kill and maim.

My two closest friends in the Guides, Betty and Muriel, were fun to be with; we loved camping trips, and working for badges. Betty was Church of England and Muriel (Mu) was Baptist.

One day Mu announced that she was going to be bap-tised. Would we like to go? I shuddered at the thought, and imagined the interior of the Baptist church. It looked dark and forbidding on the outside, and inside I could see the dark water. I thought about what it would be like to be publicly immersed. No, it would be horrible. How could she want to do such a strange thing – surely christening was enough?

Afterwards, she seemed to be so fanatical about her faith, as if she had something that I hadn't. Were all Baptists like this? When we were camping she read her Bible and prayed.

She was even thinking of becoming a missionary – it seemed such a waste of her life to me – she had brains, so why not use them? I was set on becoming a teacher – communicating knowledge and understanding, thinking, talking, being involved with people's minds. Mu seemed to be grasping at fantasies. How could she give her whole life to unreality, and even leave her family behind to go out to Bonga Bonga land, or wherever?

What was it that made her so much more involved than I was? I felt excluded, and didn't like it. Our church was nice, but just like a social club; it made me feel good when I was there, but I could forget about God all the rest of the week.

3

Confirmation of an Unbeliever

Despite my weekly attendance at church, I cannot remember anyone telling me how to become a Christian. It seemed to be assumed that because I had been christened and went to church I was a Christian.

I had been told how to become a Brownie, then a Girl Guide. I knew the rules and the law that I must promise to obey, and I had made a public commitment to the group. I had a badge to prove that I belonged.

Why was Church so vague in its call? It was friendly and sociable, but Sunday was more a day of duty than of joy. All of us were lukewarm in our commitment to God and to each other.

When I left home for University, I left Church behind.

Yet I sensed a gap in my life. Sundays weren't the same any more. But how could I believe totally unscientific things, such as the virgin birth, the resurrection of a dead body, or miracles? I was seeking the truth, and I could find no proof for any of these. Again I felt closed off from something others accepted.

I decided to visit the only girl in Hall who was a real Christian, not just a church goer, but a believer, who spoke openly about her faith. I walked up the stairs to her room. The door was shut, and as I went to knock, I heard voices and laughter inside. She was with her boyfriend. I hesitated, and walked away, not wanting to disturb them, and I never tried again.

My first teaching job was in a girls' Grammar school in Essex. I made a friend on the staff. She was older than I was, and taught Latin. Lesley rode a large motorbike, and we started spending time together. No-one wore crash helmets in those days, and the freedom of being on the back of a big bike, speeding along roads with very few cars was wonderful.

But Lesley was a committed Christian, so I argued with her, pitting my brain against hers, and getting nowhere. However hard I tried to knock down her beliefs with reason and logic, I couldn't, not because she could answer my questions, or prove I was wrong, but because of this extraordinary brick wall I kept coming up against, called faith. How could an intelligent woman refuse to listen to reason? We talked for hours, but nothing seemed to shake her.

Lesley lent me books, introducing me to C.S. Lewis, St. Francis and others, and suggested I read the gospels. I read and pondered and tried to understand what she believed. The books and the people were fascinating, but the first glimmers of truth only broke in through Lesley's example. She was always so calm and peaceful, and had a security in herself that seemed totally lacking in my life.

I became engaged to be married, and we wanted to be married at the Priory in Christchurch. However, this was outside the parish that I lived in, and it would only be possible if I became a communicant member. I would have to join the Church of England. I joined a confirmation class. It was 1954 and I was 22.

Oh dear, how I must have disrupted those classes! The vicar suggested seeing me on my own, as I refused to forgo my scientific training and swallow all the beliefs of the Church of England. No way was I going to stand up and recite the creed. I didn't believe in the virgin birth – how could anyone be conceived by the Holy Ghost? I wasn't sure about the resurrection of the dead, and what was the Holy Catholic Church? Did it include my Congregational friends and relatives? If not, I wouldn't recite it.

I fought the issues out with Lesley, the vicar, and with God. The vicar decided it was alright, that I believed enough.

When questioned closely by him, I discovered that I

did actually believe in God, and in Jesus as His Son, and that He lived and died for us. I did want to follow Him, and model my life on His.

One night I had a vision as I knelt to pray asking God to help me. It was of Jesus' feet, impaled and bleeding. I began to understand what He had suffered for me, and I wept. Was it enough? I had to be honest and truthful, even though the vicar thought it was alright. Could I be confirmed? But the desire to be married in the Priory overcame my scruples.

I felt nothing at my confirmation – the veils we had to wear on our heads were uncomfortably tight and unbecoming, and nearly everyone else was much younger than me. It was embarrassing. I felt disappointed, having assumed that something amazing would happen when the bishop placed his hands on my head.

The next Sunday I went to take my first communion, getting up early with Lesley. As I knelt waiting, I realised that this was special, but I felt totally unworthy and didn't want to go forward. How could I be included with so much unbelief in my heart and mind?

Lesley was smiling and waiting for me, what could I do? I ate the bread and drank the wine for the first time, and discovered an amazing joy and peace. God was here in this sacrament, and however little I understood or believed, He had met me. The music too – it was so familiar, from my childhood, as I knelt listening as a Girl Guide at church parade, only there because Betty, my patrol leader, expected it. The service was, after all, beautiful. I sensed a mystery and a holiness beyond the reality I believed in.

In the staff room there was rejoicing among the C. of E's that I was now one of them! I wasn't at all happy with this idea. As far as I was concerned I was still a member of the Congregational church in which I had been brought up, and to which I owed so much. I now believed that I belonged to two denominations instead of one!

Then the headmistress said, 'I am so pleased that you now believe in the Apostolic succession!'

What was she talking about? I was shattered. I hadn't changed my beliefs in anything, and no-one had mentioned that believing in the Apostolic succession was obligatory to becoming a member of the Church of England! Anyway, I still didn't believe half the creed which I said with large gaps on a Sunday! I felt a total fraud.

4

Lessons from Quakers

During the summer of 1955 I moved to Somerset to teach at Sidcot, (a Quaker boarding school) and to be near my fiancé. In the following spring I was married at the Priory. My dreams of a beautiful wedding came true.

Despite my membership of the Church of England, during my three years at Sidcot I only attended Quaker meetings.

I hadn't met Quakers before, and only had a hazy idea of what they were like, expecting them to live austere and dedicated lives, without much fun. But like any other group of people they were tremendously varied. Certainly their values were different – they did not indulge in frivolity, clothing was good and simple and was expected to last, as were the other necessities of life. Service to the community was of paramount importance.

The children were told of the dedication of those who had gone before, helping and intervening for justice, against poverty and intolerance, and prejudice. Old scholars would return from far flung places to talk of the needy, and the work that they were doing among them.

Many of the Quakers acted on what they believed, caring for the unloved, the homeless, the prisoner, the housebound, the handicapped. I was seeing Christianity in action.

Each Sunday, when on duty, I was expected to go to the morning meeting, which meant sitting in silence for an hour. I had never experienced long silences in my Congregational church, or in the Church of England. How could anyone fill their mind with thoughts of God for an hour? Maybe I could take a book? But staff had to sit in front, facing the assembled school. Somehow I would have to survive.

The meeting would be interspersed by one of the older Quakers standing and reading from the Bible, or recounting an example of God working in their lives to encourage the rest. The silences between were long, but, strangely, I began to enjoy them. I had never had this opportunity before. If I had been silent, it would be when walking in the countryside, or when listening to music. I now tried to meditate on Jesus and His life, and God's love for me.

Gradually the silences became beautiful, and the hour seemed to get shorter and shorter. Was it here that God spoke to some of those young minds, giving them the call, and the courage, for the difficult situations many of them would face in the future?

Some of the values I had unconsciously acquired began to be challenged. Perhaps simplicity of life and worship was better? Here the emphasis was not on Sunday services, but on giving all that you could (often sacrificially) to others, and leading a life of love and service in the community.

For three years I lived among and watched and listened to these people. They had their faults and failings like anyone else, but I admired and respected the principles on which their lives rested.

However, for some, brewing wine was a pastime that went with the thrifty activities of growing your own fruit and vegetables, bottling, jam-making, and pickling. We frequently got merry at evenings with our new Quaker friends, sampling their home-made wine!

Maybe there was a seriousness in these people that I hadn't encountered before, but their quietness was restful, and never threatening. They were gentle, and never tried to impose their beliefs and ideals on the children or the staff who were not Quakers. Again, it was the example of their lives that spoke the most.

The Servant Heart

There are no other hands but mine,
        no other feet,
        no other voice to speak Your love,
        no other heart to beat
and plead for those who suffer, those who die,
outside and lost from Your great plan.

        Your heart in mine must break,
        Your tears through me must weep,
        Your arms through mine embrace,
        Your voice through me should speak
against injustice, greed, the power that crushes
woman, man, or child.

        In each You long to live,
        In each to reign,
        In each to give Your peace,
        In each release from pain,
        In each Your Holy love
            to pour again.

Use now
        my feet,
        my hands,
        my voice,
        my heart.
Transform this lowly vessel, sin depart,
Pour in Your servant power
        of selfless love,
that stooping down
to wash each other's feet,
        Jesus we'll meet.

'. . . . I tell you the truth, whatever you did for one of the
least of these brothers of mine, you did for me.'
                        (Matthew 25: 40)

'*What good is it, my brothers, if a man claims to have faith but has no deeds? . . .*'

'*. . . faith by itself, if it is not accompanied by action, is dead.*'

(James 2: 14, 17)

5

Shadow of His Hand

We moved from Somerset to Welwyn Garden City, and there, in October 1960, our daughter Sally was born. I left teaching to enjoy the new experience of being a Mum.

I soon became friends with other new Mums. One of them, like me, was totally untrained for motherhood. Lorna had been a career woman, playing the violin in a big city orchestra. She was the first friend I had made who was a practising Roman Catholic.

I was now in a complete quandary as to which denomination I belonged to. I had identified so closely with the Quakers in Somerset that now I didn't seem to fit in anywhere. My husband wasn't particularly interested in going to church, so we didn't bother.

Life was busy and Sundays were welcome days off. We could work in the garden, and enjoy our new daughter. Lorna was much more devoted than I was. She had a kitchen prayer hanging up, and a crucifix, and went to mass and confession. It didn't seem to make any difference to our friendship, though we argued about contraception and obeying the Pope. I hadn't had a Catholic as a friend before and we got on well, sharing our problems over the babies that we were both so unready to care for.

Of course we had Sally christened in the local C. of E., as the family expected it. Lesley took on the job of Godmother, and I know she prayed regularly for Sally. Was that why Sally always felt so close to Jesus as a child?

It was a joint christening, with three babies and a packed church. Sally cried a lot, and I felt exhausted with night feeds, and preparing for all the visitors. It wasn't very uplifting and I didn't go to church again.

When Sally was ten months old we moved again.

Before we moved, my husband decided that he needed a new artificial eye. He lost an eye as a toddler due to a growth. What he thought was to be a routine procedure became a real shock. He was told that it had been discovered that his condition – retinoblastoma – was hereditary, and he was advised to have the eyes of any children he might have carefully checked.

I had never heard of cancer being hereditary, and couldn't believe there was anything wrong with our lovely daughter, but, just in case, we took her up to the children's hospital at Great Ormond Street to have her eyes tested.

The Doctor was abrupt and discourteous, giving her a very cursory check without using eye drops, and he said that he could find nothing wrong.

I knew little about babies, and their normal behaviour at 8–9 months, so believed that all was well, and we were caught up in the turmoil of moving home for the next few weeks.

In Milford–on–Sea I noticed that when Sally looked into the light, there was a reflection like a cat's eyes – was this normal? I checked with the nurse at the baby's clinic, and she was sure there was nothing wrong. Sally was so alert and contented. Again I was reassured.

We were looking forward to Sally's first birthday, so my mother came to stay to enjoy the occasion with us, and to see something of her little grand-daughter. As she watched Sally, playing and eating, she became concerned (I had told her nothing of our fears, not wanting to worry her unnecessarily).

'Cynthia, is there something wrong with Sally's eyes? She doesn't seem to be seeing properly.'

My heart and stomach turned over – my mum knew more about babies than I did so was the prediction about hereditary cancer correct? Immediately I rang the nearest eye hospital at Southampton arranging for Sally to see the specialist, as quickly as possible.

The diagnosis was worse than we could ever have feared. Both Sally's eyes were badly affected with cancerous growths. This time she had been properly examined with drops, and anaesthetic, so there could be no mistake.

It was impossible to believe. She seemed so fit and normal. It was as if I was asleep and having a terrible nightmare. Surely I would wake up, and find this wasn't true? The doctor could not even hold out hope that she would live. The cancer could have gone down the optic nerves, in which case we were too late.

My mother, when she saw my pain and grief, said that she wished I had never been born. She could not bear to see the suffering I was going through. Somehow that stung me. Surely, whatever happened, there had to be a reason, a purpose. Even with this I could not regret my existence.

For three days I wept constantly. Sleep was the only relief, but only to wake again to this unbelievable nightmare.

Our little daughter was oblivious to her plight, still laughing, playing and exploring. I was totally stunned with shock, unable to think clearly, under a huge burden of grief and pain. Would Sally live, and if she lived, would she be blind? Was there any hope? I could bear it no longer, I knew I must do something.

My mother had gone home. My husband was at work, and I was alone with Sally. The science that had answered all my questions before had now let me down. There was only God left.

I put Sally into her pram, and left the house. Where could I go? I tried the nearby church, which was open. Inside it seemed cold and forbidding, and there was a woman, cleaning. She watched us obviously wondering why I was there.

I couldn't talk to God there, so I walked down to the

35

sea, buying Sally a lollipop on the way. No wonder she would fret in her pram sometimes recently. She must have been bored, seeing so little.

The beach was empty. It was a cold, grey day in early November 1961. There was no-one about. I stood at the top of the beach, looking out to sea.

'God, if You are there, I'm sorry I haven't talked to You for such a long time, but I need help. I know I've never believed in miracles, but I need one, right now, and if all those stories in the Bible are true, please send a miracle. You gave me my daughter and I know You've every right to take her away from me. I accept that she could die. I can't fight it any more. If you want her, God, I give her to You. But, please God, if You would save her life, and her sight, I will give my life to You, and do whatever You ask me.'

Maybe you shouldn't bargain with God, but I was beyond caring about what you should or shouldn't do.

Then, as I stood there, it was as if a huge weight lifted from me, and as the weight lifted a deep peace started to pour over me, and, most amazing of all, my heart filled with joy.

How could I feel happiness in the middle of this nightmare? Then some words came into my mind.

'Everything is going to be alright.'

I knew that I hadn't thought those words. It was impossible in the situation, and I knew the words were from God. He had heard me, He had answered me, He really was there.

At last at 29 years of age, I knew God was real.

He cared about my pain and suffering, and had even given me peace and joy in the middle of it.

I didn't understand what the words meant. Would Sally die, or be blind? I only knew that whatever happened God would be there. The paralysis of grief and pain was gone, the numbness in my mind had disappeared, and I could think clearly and rationally again.

I remembered what the doctor had said, 'There is one

man in the world who is trying to treat this condition, a Mr. Stallard, of Morefields Eye Hospital in London.'

He had suggested that we could contact him, so I decided that I must do this straight away. I had the phone number in my diary, and some change in my purse. I found a public phone box, and rang London on my way home, explaining the situation and asking for an appointment – it was urgent. Yes, Mr. Stallard would see Sally two days ahead, on Friday, November 5th.

At Morefields Eye Hospital, Sally had drops put in to dilate her pupils, and then was taken away. We sat waiting in silence, in a corridor that was long, white and empty. Then, the sound of running feet. It was Mr. Stallard, still in his white coat, and white theatre boots. As he came towards us, I saw the tears pouring down his face. We were too late, he had never seen such a bad case. If only we had found out earlier, he could have done something. We wept.

'What can be done, is there any hope, anything you can do?' we asked.

'You must decide,' he said.

First of all he needed our permission to remove the one eye that was completely filled by the growth. Did we want him to remove the other as well, which was also badly affected? It could be risky to leave it, because he couldn't promise that the cancer hadn't gone down the optic nerve.

We had to choose, and we took the risk. If there was any chance of Sally having some sight, we wanted to take it.

We stayed in hospital as long as we could, but, in those days, mothers and fathers did not remain with their children. We left Sally and returned to Milford-on-sea, keeping in touch by phone. Sally's one eye was removed immediately. The next weekend we went back to London.

Sally, by now, had been moved to St. Bartholomew's Hospital, and had contracted gastro-enteritis, and was very ill. When I saw her alone in her cot, in isolation in a side ward, I just held her in my arms and wept. We lived so far away. If only I could be with her more. Sister Clarke, a small, bright, energetic woman, looked at us.

'Would you like to come and stay in the hospital? We could probably find a bed for you somewhere. It would help Sally's recovery.'

We agreed that I would come back in a week to stay. When I returned, Sally was in a cot in the main ward near Sister Clarke's desk. She had recovered from the gastro-enteritis. How she clung to me – I wasn't allowed away from her.

By now she was virtually blind, so I tried to amuse her with things she could touch and hold, and hear. The retina in her remaining eye was now completely detached by the growth. Mr. Stallard started chemotherapy, and slowly the sight of her eye returned. The retina started to re-attach, as the chemotherapy reduced the growth.

Then, three weeks after the operation, the results of the sectioning of the optic nerve came through. It was clear – the growth had not started to grow towards her brain. She wouldn't die.

How I thanked God. That deep reassurance was now a memory, but I clung on to it. The miracle I had bargained for was beginning.

All the treatment Sally received was experimental. She was in the first generation of children who had inherited this condition, and Mr. Stallard was pioneering its treatment, each child being treated differently. If we had been anywhere else in the country the only treatment would have been to remove both eyes.

Mr. Stallard decided to start radiation treatment, so each day Sally was given pentathol, and, when asleep, was taken to the room containing the huge machine to administer the cobalt radiation. It was a daily battle, because Sally hated the pentathol, and fought to stay awake, but the cancer was disappearing.

In January of 1962 Sally's treatment was finished, and she was allowed home, but her blood count was going down because of the radiation treatment. She had penicillin daily to counteract infections to which she would have little resistance. Each week she needed a blood test.

Then there were trips back to London to see Mr. Stallard. How thrilled he was with Sally, now with an artificial eye fitted, and the central vision saved in her other eye.

Sally had quickly learnt to compensate, and few people realised how limited her sight was. She was a real chatterbox, and Mr. Stallard loved to see her, and talk to her, and show her to his students.

How thankful we have been, for the skill and care of that great man. Even if we had been able to pay for Sally's treatment, we could not have had more courteous and caring attention.

The miracle I had asked for had taken place. 'Everything was alright,' as God had promised me. My little daughter was alive, and well, and could see.

As a result of this experience, there was now a fundamental change in my life.

Through the pain and suffering which God had allowed, I had discovered the reality of His care for me, and the truth of His existence.

> *'I know, O Lord, that your laws are righteous, and in faithfulness you have afflicted me.'*
>
> (Psalm 119: 75)

His love was so great that He had allowed this painful experience, to bring me the joy of knowing Him, a joy above all pain and suffering, and a peace in the middle of turmoil.

I began to understand real love. It was a love that could sometimes be like the healing power of the surgeon's knife. It could also be like a bridle and bit, stopping my headlong flight, and turning my life to a new direction.

> *'I will instruct you and teach you in the way you should go;* . . . .'
>
> (Psalm 32: 8)

It was only when I was at a place of total desperation that I had cried out to God, and found that He was there.

> *'I sought the Lord, and he answered me; he delivered me from all my fears.'*
>
> (Psalm 34: 4)

I must now keep my side of the bargain; my life now belonged to Him.

A Psalm

Out of deep anguish I cried to you,
Out of the depths of despair
I pleaded my cause,
That you would spare her life, her sight,
Yet she was yours, to do with as you would,
And who was I, to ask for blessings from your hand,
God of pure love, pure justice,
Awful in majesty and power.
All I could offer was my life,
That you had given to me.
Was this enough
To turn aside the pain and darkness
Swirling and choking deep within?

Your gracious kindness, Father, is beyond telling,
For you, beyond time, beyond thinking,
Came to me, lifted me out of the storm and pain,
Tenderly, gently, restored and comforted me,
Breaking the bonds round my heart
And healing my wounds.
Standing me in golden light
Surrounded by joy,
Lifting the weight over me,

40

Freeing me to trust and not be afraid,
To know that all would be well,
And all manner of things would
Indeed be well, for ever.

'He reached down from on high and took hold of me;
he drew me out of deep waters.
He rescued me from my powerful enemy,
from my foes, who were too strong for me.
They confronted me in the day of my disaster,
but the Lord was my support.
He brought me out into a spacious place;
he rescued me because he delighted in me.'

(Psalm 18: 16–19)

6

Joining the Church of England

By Sally's second birthday we had moved to our new home in a village near Lymington, and in 1963, our son Stephen was born.

I discovered that there was a Sunday school nearby, in a small chapel just down the lane, so I started taking Sally. She enjoyed going, and I felt at home in the simple building, the big windows reminding me of the chapel of my childhood.

The afternoon was organised and led by the vicar of the local Anglican church. He so obviously loved Jesus, and had a way of telling Bible stories so that they came alive for the children. The hymns were simple, and it was a pleasant and happy hour.

I joined in with the singing, and then was asked if I would join the church choir. I was hesitant because I had thought of going to the Congregational chapel in the village. I pointed out that I had a baby, and couldn't get to Evensong. Also I didn't know the Anglican services and music, as I had only attended early communion since my confirmation. The vicar didn't think this mattered – choir practice was on Friday and if I would like to come along he would be pleased. Also he asked if we would like him to come and pray round our new house. This seemed a good idea.

When he arrived we knelt in each room and prayed for God's blessing. I didn't know that such things were done by the Church. Perhaps Anglicans had some good ideas that we hadn't had in the Congregational church?

My husband didn't mind me going to sing in the choir, though he would rather stay at home. The children would be in bed on Friday evenings, and on Sunday he would look after the roast, so that I could go to morning service. If God wanted me to join this church and sing in the choir I would do so.

The choir was one of the best in the area, with a very able and dedicated choirmaster and organist. The church building was old and beautiful, and lovingly cared for. I found the music inspiring; I hadn't realised how familiar Sung Eucharist would be. Of course – the hours spent on my knees at church parade as a Girl Guide!

The service hadn't changed, but now I was part of it all, and I knew that the God we were worshipping really existed. I knew that He heard and answered prayers – that miracles did occur. Now I could say the whole of the creed truthfully – I believed it all. I knew too that there was a resurrection of the dead.

My father-in-law was a diabetic. He developed cancer, and needed an operation. We went to Wolverhampton to visit him.

Pop was very ill after the operation, and one night the family were called to the hospital. I stayed at home to look after Sally who was fast asleep in her cot. After doing a few household chores, I sat in the lounge, thinking of Pop, and hoping he would pull through. It was 9.30 p.m. when I suddenly felt a great heaviness lift from me. It was wonderful, I felt such peace and joy and I knew that he was better. I was sure that the family would soon be home with the good news that the crisis was over, and he was recovering. The telephone rang. It was my sister-in-law. She said,

'Pop is dead!'

I couldn't believe it. I was so sure that he was alright. 'When did it happen?' I asked.

'At 9.30 p.m.' she said.

Then I realised. I had misinterpreted the experience of his deliverance from pain and illness, which I had fleetingly shared. I had for some reason been able to know that when he died he was released into great joy and freedom.

> *'. . . . Death has been swallowed up in victory.'*
>
> (1 Corinthians 15: 54)

Again I could not understand why I had been allowed
to know this. Surely it would have been better for his
wife and children to have this wonderful assurance of his
happiness?

At least I could genuinely and truthfully believe now
in a life after death, not that anyone at church questioned
my beliefs. The important thing was that I could sing,
and help put on a lovely service of worship on Sunday,
for the enjoyment of God and the congregation.

The choir were a group apart – by the time we left
everyone else had gone, and we had to arrive early
to robe-up.

I had no idea where anyone in the choir or congregation
lived. (The friends I had made in the village didn't go
to church). But then this was the same as my childhood
church, so it didn't seem at all unusual to me. Religion
was a private and personal matter, not something you
talked about openly to anyone else.

But I had taken my first step towards the Body of Christ
– the Church. This was my first involvement as an adult
with other Christians. I was happy. It was wonderful to
be part of the beautiful music, and I sensed the closeness
and presence of God in the sacraments.

I enjoyed the pleasant and friendly chatter before and
after services with the rest of the choir. As my children
grew up, they would also sing in the choir, developing
their musical gifts.

> *'From him (Christ) the whole body, joined and held
> together by every supporting ligament, grows and builds
> itself up in love, as each part does its work.'*
>
> (Ephesians 4: 16)

I was unaware that Church could be different, and that
my involvement was still superficial, and I would have

44

been content to remain like this. But even bigger traumas were to come into my life, to disturb my complacency, and to bring me a new and deeper understanding of the spiritual dimension.

I had no concept of the opposing forces of good and evil. I remember that when Stephen was christened, he sneezed as the water was sprinkled onto his forehead. The vicar laughed about it afterwards, saying, 'He sneezed the devil out.' I didn't quite understand what he meant. The devil was just a joke, I assumed.

7

A Glimpse of Heaven and Hell

In the Spring of 1964 my marriage reached a crisis point. Forces were unleashed around us that were powerful and frightening.

I had dismissed the devil as a fairy story, a joke. Now I was shown that he wasn't a joke, that evil forces did exist, that we were involved in a spiritual battle.

One night I became acutely aware of this battle. I could not stay in bed, so I went and stood by the window.

I did not dare to draw the curtains back. It was completely dark, and my heart was beating fast. Outside I could hear a wild hissing noise, and in my mind's eye, could see an enormous snake-like creature circling the house.

I started to pray, and knew that I mustn't stop for an instant. 'In the name of the Father, the Son, and the Holy Spirit.' 'In the name of the Father, the Son, and the Holy Spirit.' I repeated it over, and over again. I must have stood there for at least 5 hours, from midnight till dawn, praying constantly. The last hour was the worst, as the battle seemed to intensify.

As I prayed the sweat poured from me. Then, it was over. Silence. I could have wept with relief. Whatever it was had gone.

I drew back the curtains. The sky was beginning to lighten. I went back to sit up in bed, looking out at the dawn sky. Our bedroom window was large, and faced east looking across flat fields to Beaulieu Heath. There were bare trees on the horizon. As I sat and watched, the sun began to appear behind the trees.

Slowly, everything started to change. Although I was

sitting in bed, I was no longer in the normal dimension. My eyes were opened to an unbelievable beauty. Huge flocks of birds started to fly silently across the sky, from south to north. The sun was revolving like a great ball of fire. I knew that I was close to God. It was impossible to describe. It felt like waking up from a bad dream, like coming home to where you have always wanted to be. There was no evil anywhere anymore. I was totally at one with myself, totally at one with everything else. Rapture and ecstasy were inadequate words, but that seemed to be what I was experiencing.

The sun rose above the trees. Then I knew that the experience was fading. I cried out.

'Please don't send me back. Let me stay here with You, God. I don't want to go back.'

I was desperate – the beauty and joy were slowly slipping away, I couldn't hold on to them.

'Please God, don't send me back.'

Then I saw some red spots floating before my eyes. Suddenly I knew what God was saying to me.

'Those red spots are your sins. You are not ready yet to stay with me.'

The knowledge was devastating – what could I do? How could I be free to go back one day to God? I didn't care what it cost. (I hadn't yet heard or understood the Gospel message!)

'Jesus – You died, You suffered to overcome evil. Perhaps if I offer to suffer too, I will be free of my sins?'

Nothing else mattered anymore. My whole life was now going to be dedicated to getting back to that wonderful existence.

Some days I would weep, remembering the glory and wonder. Why did I have to know of this wonderful existence? It was as if I had been on a diet of bread and water, and was then given a taste of delicious food. The bread and water now seemed dull and boring. Or, like a prisoner locked up in a cell, I had been let out to run in a beautiful place, with all the love, freedom, and

47

companionship I could ever want. How could God put me back into that prison cell again?

But, through the pain of my marriage breaking up, I could cope – I just had to remember that wonderful time. And if this pain was to purge away my sins, it was worth it. My human suffering didn't matter. Nothing mattered as much as getting back to that place with God.

During the days and weeks following, there seemed to be a radiance round all I looked at – the flowers, the trees, the sky, the people. As I walked along the streets of Lymington, everyone who passed looked so beautiful, radiating a glory I had never seen before. It didn't matter how old, or ugly – they were unbelievably beautiful. What was it Wordsworth said about 'trailing clouds of glory'? My eyes had again been opened to a 'glory in the earth'. 'The glory and the freshness of a dream' – 'every common sight . . . . apparelled in celestial light.'

(From William Wordsworth's ode, 'Intimations of Immortality.')

The new knowledge I had gained of spiritual forces battling around us, became linked to my offering of myself to God. My life now became punctuated by similar spiritual battles.

There was no-one that I could share these with, so I kept them secret. Though I would wonder if there was anyone anywhere who would understand, and who might be doing the same thing?

The battles became my private work for God – part of the repayment of my debt for the miracle He had performed. I knew great joy, as I realised that I was sharing, in a very small way, in the suffering of Jesus. Would this eventually enable me to go back to that wonderful place with God?

8

The Valley of Death

On the first day of term, in January, 1973, I arrived home to find a note on the table.

My husband had left, and he said that he would never come back. There was to be no communication between us, and he left no address.

However difficult and unsatisfactory our relationship had been, it had never occurred to me that our marriage would break up. I always believed in our love for each other, and hoped we would get through our problems.

Here was a nightmare of a different sort, first my daughter, who at the age of 8 had to go miles away to a boarding school for partially sighted children, now my husband. Was it all my fault? What had I done or not done? Why hadn't I seen this coming?

A pain and hurt entered my heart that I had never before experienced. Work became a lifeline. I went into automatic. Although everything in my heart seemed to have died, my head could still function. I could go through the motions of teaching.

At work I could tell no-one what had happened in my marriage; I would have broken down. I had to keep going, and I told no-one at church.

On the Sunday after my husband left, Stephen and I sang in the choir as usual, but no-one seemed to notice that I wasn't really there anymore, that part of me had died and I was locked up in grief. I walked outside after the service, longing for comfort.

The usual polite handshakes; no time to talk.

One person however came up to me, put his arms round me, and gave me comfort. He was a mongol –

Peter – the son of a doctor in the church. 'Was he closer to Your heart, Lord, than anyone else?'

Eight months later my husband contacted me, and told me where he was living. Perhaps it was right after all that he had left me? People warned me before our marriage that it wouldn't work. I knew that I must build my life alone.

One Wednesday in the following November I started to feel ill at work. For some time I had been suffering from giddy headaches, and, as I sat in the department drinking coffee after break, there was a strange sensation in my head. I knew that I must go home and lie down.

Somehow I drove home and staggered into bed. When Stephen came home I was able to get into the kitchen to make him some tea to eat, while he watched children's T.V. I went back to bed, then to the bathroom – violent sickness, everything went black.

I had an odd dream – it was a lovely sunny day, and I was watching a cricket match. I opened my eyes, and found that I was lying full length on the bathroom floor (had an angel lowered me down? – I had been bending over the basin!) I tried to move, and found that I couldn't. What had happened? I seemed to be paralysed.

The door was ajar. Could I get to it and call Stephen? I could move my arms, and the tiled floor was slippery, so I started to push myself along on my back. Every inch was an enormous effort. The sweat was pouring off me. Would I ever reach the door? I was exhausted, but could just push the door open and call for Stephen. Children's T.V. was finishing, so I must have been unconscious for at least 20 minutes. Stephen heard me, and ran to the bathroom. I explained to him that I couldn't move and needed help. I was very cold, so he got me a pillow and a blanket. Then I asked him to alert a neighbour. I tried not to frighten him. It was dark outside and stormy, with wind and rain. He was 9 years old and would have to go out alone. It was a long way round to the neighbours, along a dark country lane.

Eventually he managed to alert Nan who was able to drag me along on the bathroom mat, over the polished floor into the bedroom, then lift me onto the bed.

The doctor said he couldn't come out; it was probably just a migraine. But my neighbours were worried, and called two of my friends. After more phone calls the doctor at last came out. He examined me, and said that I must go straight to hospital. He wrote a long letter giving his diagnosis, but he didn't tell me what it was, though it looked serious from his behaviour and expression.

Sian (a colleague from College) took Stephen to her home, and I was carried out on a stretcher through the storm to an ambulance.

The journey to Southampton seemed endless, every bump on the road registering through my head and body. I was put into a ward in the General Hospital for two days, and not allowed to move from a prone position. On the Friday I was moved to the Neurological Unit for tests under anaesthetic.

The next day a doctor came to talk to me. He sat on my bed, saying that he needed my permission for an operation. He explained that I had suffered from a brain haemorrhage, due to an aneurism. There had been a weakness in the outer layer of the communicating artery directly under the brain. If I was willing they would operate, and clip the damaged artery. It was dangerous, but the alternative was to lead a vegetable–like existence on drugs, with no exertion or excitement. I knew there was no choice, and I must risk the operation, so I gave my permission. It was to take place as quickly as possible, on Monday.

On the Sunday, John, my vicar, and his wife, Rosemary, came to see me. They stood each side of my bed, Rosemary holding one hand and John the other. John prayed, and signed my forehead with the cross. I felt a deep peace, and knew no fear. I could trust God. If I died He would take care of my children. Perhaps I was

51

to be with Him at last, in that wonderful paradise I had glimpsed? I was unafraid of death.

My thick, long dark hair, was all shaved off, as I was prepared for the operating theatre. My church prayed for me. Sian and her husband went and knelt in the little church of St. Nicholas, in Brockenhurst and prayed during the operation.

It was a complete success. Jason Bryce and his team tunnelled under my brain, placing a metal clip on the aneurism, after removing the skull bone on the right side.

I was in a reclining position in a wheelchair. Someone was shouting at me. I opened my eyes. The operation must be over, I was alive. I was propped up on pillows with tubes everywhere – drips into my arms and drainage tubes into my skull. I could think clearly again, as if masses of cotton-wool packing had been removed from my head.

During the haemorrhage, blood had shot down the optic nerve blood vessels into my right eye, so my vision was obscured by a blood clot. The muscles at the back were paralysed, so that I saw two of everything. The eyelid would not open. Apart from that, I had no paralysis. It was only later that I discovered that I could have suffered brain damage. God had truly been guiding the surgeon's hand, and caring for me.

My bald head, with its huge yellow painted scar looked awful. On the day I came out, I went straight to a shop to buy a black curly wig! Later when my eyelid opened, I had to wear a black patch to prevent me seeing double. I looked like a pirate! When my doctor came to visit me at home he said,

'Welcome to the land of the living!'

He had only diagnosed one brain haemorrhage before, of a young man in his twenties, who had died on his way to hospital, so he hadn't expected me to survive. I knew that I was now living on borrowed time.

I looked round my house at my precious possessions,

and realised that suddenly and unexpectedly, at 41, I could have been dead! What importance would my home and garden have then? These things were of secondary importance to the eternal home that I might at any time be called to.

What sort of home was I building for myself in eternity? I realised that my earthly possessions were only of value when they could be used to express my love for God, and for other people. It was only love that would last.

'Please Lord, help me to eliminate the unnecessary and superfluous in my life, that I can give more of my time to loving and worshipping You, and to the needs of those around me. Amen.'

As a tree
so may I be,
in life,
building for death.

That when I die,
there will be wood,
for a home
in Eternity.

'. . . . I consider everything a loss compared to the surpassing greatness of knowing Christ Jesus my Lord, for whose sake I have lost all things. I consider them rubbish, that I may gain Christ . . . .'

(Philippians 3: 8)

'. . . . All men are like grass, and all their glory is like the flowers of the field. The grass withers and the flowers fall, because the breath of the Lord blows on them. . . . but the word of our God stands for ever.'

(Isaiah 40: 6–8)

53

9

Born Again

In 1978 a new technician arrived in the department. She was well qualified and very efficient. One day we were chatting together in the biology lab. It was at the end of the college day, and every one else had gone home. The conversation came round to Christianity and May questioned me about my faith. I started getting hot and uncomfortable. I didn't talk about God to anyone. Surely this was a private affair? Anyway I believed that no-one could tell me much that I didn't already know! After all God had spoken to me, transported me to a kind of seventh heaven, and performed miracles for me. I had given Him my life. Why was she talking to me as if I still didn't understand anything about Jesus? It was embarrassing, and I was quite glad when the conversation was over. She seemed totally unimpressed when I told her of my amazing experiences, and of my relationship with God!

Next day, when I got home from work, and opened my college bag, I found a book inside, called 'Nine o'clock in the morning'. It had May's name in it. Why had she put this book into my bag without saying anything? I hoped she wasn't afraid of me! Anyway the book looked quite interesting, so I started to read it.

I became intrigued and amazed. Did things like this really happen today? Were people walking about doing the things that Jesus did? I had never heard of being baptised in the Spirit, or of Pentecostals and charismatics. What a shame that Seattle was such a long way off – it would be wonderful if that sort of thing happened in England. But were people actually speaking in tongues today? I thought that gift was only meant for the early disciples, and I knew nothing about the Holy Spirit. To me He was just a name which we tacked on to the end of our prayers.

Anyway, I now realised that this being 'born again' experience had never happened to me. Yes, I had given my life to God, but I was still in charge of it! Do people really ask Jesus to take over? Do they actually ask Him to come into their lives and tell them what to do all the time? Oh dear, He might ask you to give up things you enjoyed, and then want you to do things you didn't enjoy! But in the book it all sounded so wonderful. I wished that I could go to Seattle, where it was all happening, and meet some of those people who could speak in tongues, and who could heal people through prayer, and perform miracles.

I returned the book. I had enjoyed reading it.

May told me that she and her husband were going to be baptised. Whatever for? Surely they'd been christened? They were adults, with children of their own, so it seemed really odd. They even thought that God had told them to be baptised, though they weren't sure why.

I was curious about baptism, recalling the memories of my teenage friend Mu being baptised, and my childish fears of the whole idea. Perhaps I would go along and watch? This new technician was different somehow, and it could be interesting. It would mean missing morning service that day, but I got permission from the vicar to go and May seemed pleased.

The small Baptist church was full when I arrived. I found a seat on my own by the central aisle, near the back. I didn't recognise anyone there. I could see May and Reg sitting in the front row. Reg was wearing a short sleeved white suit, and May was in a long white dress.

The morning service was very similar to that of the Congregational church I had attended as a child, so I felt quite at home. The baptistry was at the front of the church on the left hand side, and you walked down some

55

steps into it. I wondered if I would be able to see them being baptised, and thought that I should have sat nearer to the front. After some rousing hymns and prayers it was time for the baptism.

Apparently Reg and May would first of all speak to the congregation. I was then amazed by the sight of our new technician, standing in front of a church full of people, telling them of her love for God and Jesus, and why she was being baptised. As I watched, her face was lit up like an angel's. The tears came to my eyes, and started to roll down my cheeks. Oh dear, why was I always so emotional? Then Reg spoke. I could see little of their baptism, but I had a really good view of them sharing their testimony.

We stopped for coffee and biscuits afterwards, in a hall at the back of the church. It had been an extraordinary and powerful experience, and I still felt very strange and tearful. We went home, and they invited me to call in later to see them.

We lived in the same road, so that afternoon I went down to talk to them. They told me more about their faith and their love for Jesus, and also about being filled with the Holy Spirit. Apparently this had happened to them both, and they could both speak in tongues! I would have loved to hear them, what would it sound like? I was too polite to ask. Again I felt tearful, though neither of them seemed to notice, or be disturbed by this.

I left them to attend Evensong which was always so beautiful. There were fewer people than in the morning, and we enjoyed the gentle quietness and peace of the service at the end of the day.

As I left the church I was handed a copy of the Winchester Churchman, the diocesan newsletter, which came out every month. I opened it when I was back home, going straight to the central page – entitled 'The Rose window'. There was always an article by Bishop John Taylor here, which was by far the best part of the leaflet. I read it and found that John was talking about the Church, and our need to become more alive and active, like the early Christians. One sentence in particular caught my attention.

'Pentecostals and charismatics are an example to us all'. Up to this point I had been hesitant. I belonged to the Church of England, and maybe they didn't approve of the baptism in the Spirit? I didn't want to do anything which would damage my church membership. But John Taylor was head of our diocese – if he believed that Pentecostals were an example to us all, surely we should follow their example?

At 11pm on that Sunday, I sat in bed, thinking over the day's events. I realised that May could do something that I couldn't do. I couldn't possibly stand in front of a church full of people, and talk about my love for God. In fact I couldn't talk about God to anyone, not even my best friends – I would be far too embarrassed. It had never mattered before, but now I realised how selfish this was. People might be helped through knowing about my experiences.

Why couldn't I communicate my beliefs? I could stand up every week in front of the whole College and talk about almost anything else. It must be because I wasn't 'born again', like May and Reg, and I didn't have the gifts of the Spirit to help me as they did. I had to face it – I needed to ask Jesus into my life to change me.

A strange conversation then began in my head. There seemed to be two voices. One was persuading me that I needed Jesus, and the other that it was a bad idea – that I had managed to run my own life up to now, and being 'born again' would make life difficult. But the memory of May's and Reg's testimony kept coming back. Yes, I wanted what they had. I was going to do it.

'Please Jesus, come into my life. I want to be born again, I want You to take over from now on. I've already given You my life, but now I want to go Your way, and not my own.'

Well I wondered if that was alright. Had Jesus heard

57

me? Then I remembered about the Holy Spirit. I might as well have everything that was going!

'And Jesus, I want to be baptised in the Holy Spirit, so please come into me, Holy Spirit, and fill me.'

I wasn't expecting what followed – tears started to pour down my face, and joy filled me, flooding me from top to toe. I was ecstatic. This was wonderful. Jesus had come into me, and so had the Holy Spirit. I must now be 'born again'.

Could I pray in tongues? I tried, but nothing happened. The joy and peace were real though, and I slept deeply, waking wonderfully happy and light-hearted! I went downstairs for breakfast, and to go to College. I picked up my cigarettes and lighter – no I didn't want those any more, they went into the bin. The desire for cigarettes had totally gone. I haven't smoked a cigarette since.

I wonder if my students noticed the difference? I was bubbling with joy and happiness all day.

That evening I started to read another book which May had given me. It was about Baptism in the Holy Spirit. Perhaps I could find out how to pray in tongues? On the Tuesday evening as I read more of this book, I reached a section where it described all the things that might prevent us from speaking in tongues, and from being released into the other gifts of the Spirit.

I went down the list, mentally checking each item. No, I hadn't ever dabbled in witchcraft, the occult, spiritualism. (I had been addicted to reading horoscopes, but had given that up). I decided it wasn't anything on the list that was stopping me. But then I realised that God was asking me to think again. I went back down the list. 'Have you forgiven everyone who has hurt you?' Oh yes, I was a very forgiving person! But no, I couldn't go on – what was God trying to say to me?

'Have you really forgiven your husband for leaving you?'

Well, I thought I had. I'd been quite nice about everything, agreeing to all his requests, selling the house, encouraging him to see the children, dividing all our goods equally, and not going to a solicitor. Then I remembered – secretly, when I knew things weren't going very well for him, I was glad. After all, he had made me terribly unhappy, and had left me with all the responsibility for the children and home, living alone in a remote place in the countryside. He deserved to suffer too!

Oh dear! Of course, that was wrong. I knew that I must repent and start to pray for him, and to ask God to bless him. I couldn't feel any love for him, but I knew Jesus loved him, so I asked Jesus to give me His love for him, as I had none left of my own – I was willing to love him again.

As I prayed for him to be blessed, I found a new, strange language pouring from my lips. It was beautiful. I felt like a bird let out of a cage. My spirit was communicating with God. The language went on flowing till I finally went to sleep.

'. . . . *if the Son sets you free, you will be free indeed.*'

(John 8: 36)

'. . . . *I am the light of the world. Whoever follows me will never walk in darkness, but will have the light of life.*'

(John 8: 12)

10

Breaking and Baptism

In June 1981 I went to a meeting in Bournemouth where Colin Urquhart was to be the speaker. I had read his book, 'When the Spirit comes', and it had inspired me to pray constantly for St. John's. During morning service and evensong, and when I could visit the church alone, I prayed for the Holy Spirit to come and move among the leaders and congregation.

When I tried to share with them my new found joy and excitement in knowing Jesus and the Holy Spirit, I was regarded with some suspicion. Efforts were made to bring me back to the established conventions of the Church of England. All I could do was pray. Any attempts to take away what I now knew to be true failed. My knowledge of the Bible was very limited, but the Holy Spirit gave me a wisdom and understanding that astounded me.

'Why did this happen to me, Lord?' I would ask. 'Wouldn't it have been better to open the eyes of one of the important people in the church? Who is going to listen to a woman who only sits in the choir singing alto each Sunday?'

Another woman in the choir knew what I was talking about. Many years earlier, in 1938, Ann Harvey had been completely healed at a tent meeting in Southampton. She had been bed-ridden for four years with rheumatic fever. When she married in 1935, she was barely able to walk about, and she was told that having children would be impossible. A neighbour had taken her to this meeting, though Ann thought that she was only going shopping.

The meeting was held in a big marquee that had been erected in the park near Plummers. It was the last night that Pastor Jeffreys from America would be there. As he laid hands on her head and prayed for her, she said she felt a red hot surge go through her body; she was gloriously healed, and she returned to care for her husband and home, and shortly afterwards to have a family. Ann knew that God could work supernaturally through the power of the Holy Spirit.

Yet Ann, too, was not an important member of the church. She did the cleaning for the vicar and his wife, and was the one who helped with the teas at church bazaars and socials. I was glad though of her gentle and understanding heart, and the sympathy she gave me in my lonely situation.

I had so much wanted to share my joy with John, my vicar, but he hadn't understood about my encounter with the Holy Spirit. John really loved and knew Jesus, and I don't think he realised that most of his congregation didn't know Jesus in the same way. I would wonder what John meant when he talked of Jesus as a friend who walked beside us. I often wished that I could experience such a closeness to Jesus myself.

At last I understood. Now whenever I went into my study, which had always seemed a lonely and empty room, I discovered Jesus and the Holy Spirit were always there before me. I would never be lonely again. I had Jesus walking beside me, just as He did with John, and I also had the Holy Spirit within me to guide and help me.

Perhaps at the meeting in Bournemouth Colin Urquhart would show me what I should be doing to bring the Holy Spirit to St. John's? I took a friend with me from the congregation. Joy didn't understand what I was talking about, but she was prepared to listen. I had met Joy in the church tent at the New Forest Show, where we had both volunteered to sell books. Joy also really knew and loved Jesus. I would visit her in Brockenhurst, and sit by her warm log fire, drinking tea from delicate bone china cups. We would pray together for St. John's. Maybe Joy

61

would be filled with the Holy Spirit, and could join me on my quest to change St. John's?

Colin was an extraordinary and powerful preacher. He didn't stand up in the pulpit, but stood in the centre of the chancel, without any written notes to follow. The words poured out from him, and then he knelt down in front of the whole congregation, and, holding out his arms, he pleaded with us to lose our pride, and to humble ourselves before God! I had never seen anything like it – the effect was electric, and absolutely no-one was dozing off, or thinking about other things!

He suggested that we needed to ask God to break us. If we did this, he said, it was a prayer that would be answered more quickly than any other we had ever prayed. I thought about what he was saying. I had always hated criticism, and always liked to be the one to know the right answer in any situation. I knew I needed to pray that prayer – my pride needed to be broken.

At the end of the meeting we all stood up, holding hands across the aisles, and I prayed to be broken.

Normally after one of these meetings I would be dancing along the pavements. This time it was different. I didn't want to talk, and sat quietly in the car. Everything felt wrong. I got home and prepared for bed, wondering why I felt so strange. I knelt to pray, and then God started to speak to me.

A story formed in my head.

I had a very dear friend, who was kinder, and more loving towards me than anyone else in the world. I was very attached to this friend, who was completely trustworthy, and would always be there when I needed help. I loved this friend dearly. One day my friend was falsely charged and put into prison. He had done nothing wrong, and I was heartbroken. Then I discovered that in prison he was suffering terrible pain and torture at the hand of his accusers. What could I do? My grief for my friend was agonising. Why had this happened to him? I couldn't understand it.

'Please tell me, Father,' I said. And God did tell me. He said,

'Your friend is in prison and suffering because of you. It is your fault that he is there!'

Suddenly I understood what God was saying to me. The friend was Jesus, and although I knew He had died for my sins, somehow I had been remote from the actual process. Jesus in my mind had been put on the cross 2,000 years ago by some Roman soldiers. Now, God was showing me that I was responsible – I had taken the nails and hammered them into Jesus, I was the cause of His pain and grief. My sin had nailed Him to the cross.

What could I do? For the first time in my life I felt desperately ashamed of myself. My guilt was terrible – I had to hide. I curled up as small as possible in the corner of the room, but it was hopeless, there was nowhere I could go, and nothing I could do to escape from God. I was guilty, and I deserved to be punished. But as I wept at this horrible realisation, the words of a hymn came into my mind.

'Rock of ages cleft for me,
Let me hide myself in Thee . . .'

God is merciful, He was reminding me that there was one place that I could hide – in the broken side of Jesus. The gaping wound that I had inflicted was my only refuge from God's rightful anger. It was almost beyond my understanding. How could anyone love me that much? What friend would allow me to put them through agony, so that I could be safe? Whether I understood or not, I ran into that hiding place away from the terrible guilt I felt.

At last I was safe; Jesus' body was my shield, my protection, from my justly deserved punishment. How desperately sorry I was that I had hurt Jesus so terribly, how unbelievably thankful that His love now held me and covered me. I never wanted to hurt Him again, and for

63

the first time in my life I really repented. When I was born again two years previously, I had said I was sorry for my sins, but the words had meant very little. Now I really meant them, from my heart.

Shortly after this, on July 5th 1981, I again went to a baptism in New Milton. By now I was used to baptisms, and wasn't expecting any surprises.

Bill Miles the minister, would be leaving New Milton in a few weeks for another church. As he preached he looked around the congregation and said, 'I believe God is telling me that before I leave, there will be another baptism here.' As he said this, he looked straight at me. I was stunned – was God suggesting that I should be baptised? I had been christened and confirmed in the Church of England, so surely it wasn't necessary?

That night I couldn't sleep, and at 5 a.m. I got up, and picked up my Bible. Every page I looked at mentioned either repentance, water, or baptism. I sat and thought, and prayed,

'Please guide me Lord. I need to know clearly what You want me to do.'

As I waited quietly, God spoke to me,

'Be washed in the waters of repentance that you may be healed, that you may be free. Witness for Me.'

I knew then that God didn't just want me to be baptised, but that my lifetime of silence about God's hand on my life was to be broken. He was asking me to give my testimony in public – it was even worse than I had thought!

What should I do? I would have to get in touch with Bill Miles. Maybe he wouldn't baptise me as I was a member of the Church of England? I went to College, but my usual happy and absorbing time in the laboratory with my students was disturbed – I couldn't concentrate, and felt restless. It was no good and by 9.30 a.m. I knew I must phone.

I laid a fleece, 'Lord, if Bill answers the phone I will

ask him to baptise me, but if he doesn't, I'll assume that this restlessness isn't from You.'

Well I knew Monday was Bill's day off – hopefully he would be out or his wife would answer the phone. The possibility of Bill answering the phone was fairly small. Maybe I wouldn't have to be baptised after all, and it was all in my imagination?

The phone rang in Bill's house – I waited, it was picked up. Oh no, it was Bill answering, so I would have to ask him.

'Bill, it's Cynthia. Would you baptise me before you leave New Milton?'

'Why yes, I would be glad to,' he replied, 'as long as your vicar will give his permission.'

I didn't know how John, my vicar, would react to my request, but I did know an immediate peace and joy, and a certainty that I had done what God wanted. I returned to my class with a real happiness, and lightness of heart. Bill had agreed to baptise me, and I knew it was from God.

When I saw John he was a little puzzled by my request, but agreed to my baptism. I would have loved John to baptise me, and he did say that there was a baptistry in the diocese which we could have used. But under the circumstances, he thought it would be easier for me to use the facilities in New Milton, if Bill was willing.

The date was fixed for August 16th 1981, which was Bill's last Sunday in New Milton. After my earlier reluctance, I now felt impatient to be baptised – how would I get through the five weeks of waiting? I started to think about what I would say, and constantly went over in my mind the terror of standing up in public, and giving my testimony. Then I read in Luke, chapter 21 verses 14, 15.

'. . . . *make up your mind not to worry beforehand how you will defend yourselves, for I will give you words and wisdom . . . .*'

Jesus was telling the disciples how He would help them to witness to kings and governors. My situation wasn't quite the same, but I knew as I read Jesus' words that He was saying them to me. He wanted me to trust Him for the words I would speak.

So I made up my mind not to think again about what I was to say, and, for the last two weeks before my baptism, I rebuked Satan every time I started to think about my testimony. I was determined to rely completely on the Holy Spirit.

Then a few days before my baptism, I went down with a bad attack of 'flu. On the Friday I was confined to bed, with a high temperature and painful throat, etc. This was the middle of August! I couldn't believe it, and knew that I was under attack. Satan didn't want me to be baptised, so I told him that even if I was dying I would be there on Sunday, so he might as well give up, as he was wasting his time! On the Saturday I felt well enough to go shopping and to prepare for the next day, and by Sunday my symptoms had virtually disappeared!

I woke to a lovely sunny day, and was glad that my children and friends would be coming with me to the Church. I was the only candidate for baptism, so my family and friends could all occupy the front rows. After changing into a long white dress I sat waiting for the moment when Bill would call me forward. At last – this was it!

I felt strangely numb as I walked up the steps – remembering to hold up my dress, and not to trip over. I was facing the microphone – at least that was a familiar experience. Bill started to question me about my faith, and my wish to be baptised, and I replied, explaining how God had led me to this moment. The words poured out. I felt absolutely nothing, almost as if someone else was standing there speaking.

At one point I glanced down at the front row, and was surprised to see that nearly everyone was crying! Whatever for? I felt no emotion at all. I must have spoken for at least 10 minutes.

Then came the moment of baptism. The baptistry was

steaming! The water was really hot! (They knew I had been ill and didn't want me to be chilled.) As I entered the water, my dress floated up – why hadn't I thought to weight it down? So much for my vanity! Bill was there beside me, and plunged me under the water, baptising me in the name of the Father, the Son, and the Holy Spirit. Although I was a good swimmer, I hated having my head under water. But this time it was beautiful and the few moments I was under the water seemed to stretch into an eternity. I felt as if I was moving across space and time, from one dimension to another. I knew without a doubt, that my desire to die to myself, to die with Jesus, would truly result in a new life, which would last for ever.

I came up spluttering, having forgotten to keep my mouth shut, but it felt like heaven around me, as everyone sang joyfully. Bill had let me choose the hymns. As well as 'Rock of ages, cleft for me', we had 'To God be the glory', 'Oh for a thousand tongues to sing', and 'Alleluia, sing to Jesus'. The church was packed for Bill's last day, and the singing was wonderful. Bill's sermon was inspired and powerful and I was filled with great joy and peace.

As I said to Bill afterwards, it had been a milestone in my life. I couldn't understand why he and his wife fell about laughing. I had forgotten Bill's surname!

So here I was, christened and confirmed in the Church of England, brought up in the Congregational Church, baptised in the Baptist Church, and a member of a Church of England choir! I was also attending inter-denominational meetings in Christchurch and Bournemouth, and had enjoyed two Bible weeks at the South Downs, tasting the freedom of worshipping with Spirit-filled believers.

At last I understood the Gospel message. As I went down under the waters of repentance my sins were washed away. I didn't have to work any more to remove those red spots that had floated before my eyes, after my experience of heaven, seventeen years ago. I was free. Jesus had paid the price for me. I was definitely going back to that wonderful existence. Yippee! – what joy, what blessed assurance. My sins that had been as scarlet were now whiter than snow. Alleluia.

> '*For it is by grace you have been saved, through faith – and this not from yourselves, it is the gift of God – not by works, so that no-one can boast.*'
> (Ephesians 2: 8, 9)

> '. . . *we have confidence to enter the Most Holy Place by the blood of Jesus, by a new and living way opened for us through the curtain, that is, his body.*'
> (Hebrews 10: 19, 20)

11

The Community Church

Two weeks before my baptism I went to a Downs Bible week. It was like heaven on earth, seeing the love expressed in families and among friends, hearing the singing and worship from tent and caravan, noticing people praying openly, either alone in the early morning, or together, the families blessing and sharing their food at mealtimes, and the children, free to run about, rarely crying or fighting.

In the evening, meetings were held in a big marquee and displayed the powerful presence of God in the worship. The teaching was inspired. There were prophecies and tongues, and signs and wonders followed as people were healed and released.

We packed up sadly; all over for another year. But, what a surprise – on our way home through the Forest, only two miles from Brockenhurst was a sign – 'Bible Week'. We couldn't believe our eyes! Had we gone all the way to Plumpton for a Bible week, only to find there was to be one on our own doorstep?

May and I decided to cycle to the camp, and find out what was happening. As we dismounted, a man came towards us. He was courteous and helpful. We learnt that the church holding the camp was called the Southampton Community Church, but the meetings were open to anyone, and we could just turn up with our friends.

Our informant's name was John Mason, and he invited us to tea or coffee in his tent before or after the meetings, saying that his wife Janet would be pleased to meet us. There was a twinkle in his blue eyes as he spoke to us, and a warm friendliness in his manner. We felt happy and excited cycling home. The camp hadn't started yet, so we had time to alert the group of women who met weekly for prayer in May's home.

What was this Community Church like? May and Reg were getting restless at the thought of Bill leaving the Baptist church, and believed that God might want them elsewhere. I had no intention of leaving St. John's but needed my hunger for Spirit-filled worship and teaching satisfied. Perhaps we would all find what we were looking for at this Bible week?

We attended some of the evening meetings. They were very like the ones at Downs week, the same joy and freedom, people lifting their arms to worship, clapping, jigging up and down, singing in wonderful harmonies the spontaneous music from the Spirit, the same meaty teaching, an hour deeply involved in the Bible, expounding the word of God. The women looked rather peasant-like, with scarves tied round their heads, but no-one seemed to mind our lack of head coverings.

May and Reg wanted to get more involved with this church, so they decided to attend the meetings which were held in Totton, Southampton on Sunday afternoons, and on Wednesday evenings. I was busy with my College work and my commitment to St. John's, but thought it would be nice to occasionally go along with May and Reg. Was this alright? Was I being disloyal to my Christian family at St. John's? I prayed and sought God, and He spoke to me.

'My Body is one,
Be united in love with all Christians.
Do not seek to be confined in one group,
but go freely where I send you,
trusting only in Me, and in My guidance.
Be an ambassador, not seeking a home in this world,
for your home is with Me in heaven.
Like a bird do not be imprisoned in your nest,
but use the wings of the Spirit which I have given you,

70

to fly at My bidding.
For I have a plan to unite all who follow Me,
and you are to be part of that united body.
Trust in Me, that I will provide,
Seek only My face, and all else will be added to you.
Worship Me.'

This word was confirmed to me, as I picked up my Bible,
and read 2 Corinthians chapter 5 verse 20.

*'We are therefore Christ's ambassadors, as though God
were making his appeal through us . . . .'*

And then Jesus' prayer for all believers in John chapter
17 verses 20–23:

*'. . . I pray . . . . that all of them may be one Father, just
as you are in me and I am in you. May they also be in us
so that the world may believe that you have sent me. I have
given them the glory that you gave me, that they may be one
as we are one: I in them and you in me. May they be brought
to complete unity to let the world know that you sent me and
have loved them even as you have loved me.'*

I thought about what God had said. I was to be united
in love with all Christians, from every denomination.
They were all my family, my brothers and sisters. I would
be part of every denomination. The Church of Christ
could be one in me. I was to be a member of Jesus' united
Church. Anyone who loved Jesus I would love, I would
pray and worship with, I would fellowship with and I
would work with for the coming in of God's Kingdom.

What did all the theology, doctrines, and dogmas,
discussions, arguments and divisions matter? That was
all in the mind, which is prone to deception. But who can
deceive the heart that is in love with Jesus? What Christian can resist loving and being close to those on fire with
Jesus' love, and those who put God's Kingdom of love,
God's holiness and righteousness first in their lives?

Maybe I was being very naive. I knew nothing of the
problems between denominations. But God had spoken

to me, and I believed Him. If it was His plan to unite all His followers it was going to happen, and I intended to be part of it!

So in September 1981 I felt comforted and reassured by God's word to me. After all I had no-one else to turn to – I was alone. My decisions had to come from God and not from man. However in March 1981, a godly leader of the Church had spoken similar words to me in a letter. John Taylor, Bishop of Winchester, had come to Brockenhurst College to talk to the students in one of the weekly lectures I organised. In the second paragraph of his letter he wrote,

'I pray especially that you may always have the courage and humility to allow the extraordinary freedom of the Holy Spirit to remain free.' And in the last paragraph,

'So keep your freedom, and go on being your true self as God has made you and is making you, learning from others, and sharing with them, but never becoming stereotyped or in bondage.'

Bishop John's letter had already prepared the way for the struggle I was about to face. My contact with the Community Church brought me up against teachings that seemed to contradict Bishop John. They believed in the submission of women to men, and of everyone to the elders and leaders. What was I to believe? Was it right that I should obey other people? I felt restless and unhappy. I sought God and He answered me.

'I am the Lord your God,
I have made all things,
I hold you in My hand,
I have prepared your way to walk before Me.
    Obey Me.
For I have loved you before time began,
    and into eternity.
Seek not an earthly rule for your life,
Seek not those to obey, only those who guide.
For I am not a Shepherd who rules,

but one who leads.
Only follow where you see Me leading,
and I will call you, you will hear My voice.
There is no authority but Mine,
which I have given to all who truly turn to Me.
    Take that authority.
It can only shine from a broken and humble vessel,
    emptied of self.
Gently lead My lambs.
For he would be greatest who is the servant of all.
In the lowly and meek do I live.
Look for Me, not among the leaders of men,
    but among those who serve.'

The Lord led me to nine scriptural confirmations.

'I, even I, am the Lord . . . .'   (Isaiah 43: 11)

'See, I am sending an angel ahead of you to guard
you along the way and to bring you to the place I
have prepared.'

(Exodus 23: 20)

'Blessed is the man who makes the Lord his trust, ...'
(Psalm 40: 4)

'I am the good shepherd; I know my sheep, and my
sheep know me.'

(John 10: 14)

'. . . . his sheep follow him because they know his
voice.'

(John 10: 4)

'Humble yourselves, therefore, under God's mighty
hand . . .'

(1 Peter 5: 6)

'Your attitude should be the same as that of Christ
Jesus: Who . . . . who made himself nothing, taking
the very nature of a servant, ...'

(Philippians 2: 5–7)

> '. . . *God opposes the proud but gives grace to the humble.*'
>
> (1 Peter 5: 5)

> '. . . *I live in a high and holy place, but also with him who is contrite and lowly in spirit . . . .*'
>
> (Isaiah 57: 15)

So I understood that I was to look for God's guidance, help and counsel from the lowly and meek, and those with serving hearts. Their age, their standing in the Church or the world, whether they were male or female, black or white, was totally unimportant. What mattered was how much of the selfless love and humility of a servant they showed in their lives. I realised that I would need a deeper humbling and emptying if I was going to bring God's help and counsel to others.

At the next meeting I attended of the Community Church, there was teaching on the need for a head covering for women, when worshipping and praying in public. Somehow I couldn't accept that this was really necessary.

At St. John's I was robed from the neck down to wrists and ankles. In the Community Church I could expose my arms and legs, but not my head! Were these rules from God, or from man? I needed to know the answer. Again God spoke to me.

'Be holy as I am holy says the Lord your God.
For I look into the heart, where lie the hidden things.
And there I see the uncleanness that no outward washing
    can remove.
There I see the proud thoughts, the unrepentant ways,
that no external humility can erase.
I look not at the outward signs, for these are passing.
Only in the heart is true humility, true submission to
    My authority,
true repentance, and true love.

74

And, as these spring forth from the heart, so the
   outward signs appear,
of love, gentleness, kindness, patience.
meekness, and true humility.
Seek only to please Me in your heart.
But be not a stumbling block to those who need
                                        outer signs.
To some, a candle on an altar is My light.
To others, a headdress on a woman is My authority,
or a building made with hands, My temple.
Yet My authority covers only the heart.
My light shines only from the heart,
and My temple lies in the heart,
Seek only to please Me in your heart,
for that is all I desire from you.
Be a living witness of My love.
For I am the Alpha and the Omega,
He who is, and who was, and who is to come,
The Almighty.'

Again there were five immediate scriptural confirmations.

> 'But just as he who called you is holy, so be holy
> in all you do; for it is written, "Be holy, because
> I am holy."'
>
> (1 Peter 1: 16)

> 'You are already clean because of the word I have
> spoken to you.'
>
> (John 15: 3)

> '. . . God does not judge by external appearances. . . .'
> (Galatians 2: 6)

> 'Don't you know that you yourselves are God's temple
> and that God's Spirit lives in you?'
>
> (1 Corinthians 3: 16)

> 'For wisdom will enter your heart . . . .'
>
> (Proverbs 2: 10)

75

Yes, it was all unnecessary, and from man. How foolish and vain we are to think that we can impress God with either our clothing, furniture, or buildings.

But God had told me that even though it was His authority over my heart that He was looking for, I was not to be a stumbling block. It would make my new Christian brothers and sisters unhappy if I didn't wear a headscarf, just as it would upset them all at St. John's if I didn't put on the long purple robe to sing in the choir, and bow to the altar as we processed in.

I went out and bought several headscarves to match all my outfits. Well God had made the world very beautiful, and I was part of it. I wanted to look as attractive in these headscarves as possible! Even today, when headscarves are no longer worn, I am known by some of my friends as a person to turn to for the right scarf to wear on a special occasion!

Perhaps I should explain at this point, that before being 'born again' in June 1979, I had spent little time reading the Bible. After this date I read the Bible with a hunger and enjoyment that amazed me. As May bought the 'Every Day with Jesus' daily notes, I did too.

So when God gave me these words and scriptures, I was a Bible scholar of 16 months, fed by E.D.W.J. notes! Most of what God said to me, and the scriptural confirmations, were completely new to me. I could not have found any of the Bible references unaided.

In December 1981, May and Reg accepted membership into the Community Church. I had been going with them to the foundation classes, which explained the spiritual basis and teaching of the Church. I had really enjoyed these classes, and saw that the teaching was sound and good; I could accept it. But when Ken Ford the leader of the Totton branch of the Southampton Church, asked me if I would become a committed member, I said 'No.'

12

Joining the Community Church

At the end of 1981, Stephen and I went to Devon, and enjoyed a lovely farmhouse Christmas in an old, thick-walled stone cottage, warmed by an enormous log fire. The hills and river nearby were beautiful in the winter sunshine.

When we returned, Stephen spent the New Year with his Dad, while I 'saw in' 1982 alone, and in prayer. I was reaching a crisis point in my life, and I needed to start the year calling out for God's guidance and help, and being reassured by His love and presence with me.

A new book had just come out by Arthur Wallis, which was called, 'The Radical Christian'.[1] I remembered seeing Arthur, and hearing him speak, at the Downs and New Forest Bible Weeks, so I bought his book. As I read it, some of the words seemed to have a special significance for me – I jotted them down in my notebook.

> 'When you are persecuted in one place, flee to another.'
> 'Reluctance to allow the sword to cut them free fully and forever from the legalism of their past, prevents them reaching a dying world with the gospel.'
> 'We should be asking which is the right way – to come out, or stay in. To obey is better than sacrifice.'

[1] The Radical Christian, Copyright © 1981 Arthur Wallis, published by Kingsway Publications, Eastbourne.

'The place of God's anointing is the place of God's appointing.'
'Make sure that you are moving with God.'
'Determine that you too will obey God, commit your cause to God, and wait for Him to act.'

My efforts to bring a new awareness of the Holy Spirit to St. John's were coming under opposition. In the prayer and discussion groups, my appeals were rejected, and my suggestions argued against. But I was reluctant to allow the 'sword to cut me free!' I did not want to ask God whether I should 'come out' of St. John's or 'stay in' – I feared His answer!

Arthur's words spoke to me. 'Determine to obey God'. Was I holding out on what God wanted for me? There was only one way to find out – I must ask God. So in real turmoil of heart and mind I prayed. This was His answer.

'Peace, be still, says the Lord, for I know your heart, and I
    know your love for those at Boldre,
and I will not separate you from what is needful.
But, indeed, it is I that you need, and it is the freedom of
    My Spirit that will truly bless you.
And My longing to be poured out through you cannot be
    fulfilled until you are free of old trappings and
    old ways.
Indeed it now seems hard, but then you will know
    the joy
    of obedience to My will for your life.
So be ye separate, and put aside your old life, that
    you may
    sing a new song with my heavenly choirs.
Come out from among them into my light. I will prepare
    your path to walk in, and you will be truly blessed, as I
    freely use you, for My divine purposes.
Fully partake of the water of life, which I can only pour
    into an open vessel, held up and ready, not bound

down and closed in formality and tradition.
Do not be afraid, for I will bind up all wounds, and
loneliness and crying will be no more.
For I am the Lord who loves you, beyond your powers
of understanding, both now and into Eternity.'

God also spoke to me through His word.

> '. . . . Free yourself from the chains on your neck, O
> captive Daughter of Zion.'
>
> (Isaiah 52: 2)
>
> 'Therefore come out from them and be separate, says
> the Lord . . . .'
>
> (2 Corinthians 6: 17)
>
> 'Neither do men pour new wine into old wineskins. If
> they do, the skins will burst . . . No, they pour new
> wine into new wineskins, and both are preserved.'
>
> (Matthew 9: 17)
>
> 'Do not suppose that I have come to bring peace to the
> earth. I did not come to bring peace, but a sword.'
>
> (Matthew 10: 34)
>
> 'For the Lamb at the centre of the throne will be their
> shepherd; he will lead them to springs of living water.
> And God will wipe away every tear from their eyes.'
>
> (Revelation 7: 17)
>
> 'But my righteous one will live by faith. And if he
> shrinks back, I will not be pleased with him.'
>
> (Hebrews 10: 38)

God was asking me to leave St. John's. As He spoke to
me, I saw a picture of a jug held down by cobwebbed
thongs. It could not be picked up and emptied. Then
I saw the same jug freed from the thongs, full to over-
flowing, and God's hand reaching down to pick it up,
and pour out the water.

It was difficult to talk to John Hayter, because he was

always busy, so I decided to write to him, and explain what was happening to me. John was a godly and humble man, a servant of us all. I knew I could listen to him. He wrote in reply, saying that he understood. I must do what I believed was right, even though it would sadden him. He would go on praying for me. I was so grateful for his love and understanding.

But despite all this, I hesitated! My daughter was to be married in July at St. John's, and John would officiate. Sally was still a member of the choir, though only at home in the holidays from Derby, where she was training in occupational therapy. Traditionally the whole choir would be there for her wedding. I could not ruin my daughter's wedding day.

I was also finding it difficult to fit in socially with this new group of Christians. With only a few exceptions the adults were all in their 20's and 30's with young families. None of the women had careers; they stayed at home, looking after their husbands and children. I was an older, divorced woman, living alone with my 18 year old son, and I had a demanding full-time career. At the end of meetings I could find no-one to talk to. I would stand alone near groups or couples, hoping to be included in the conversation, but I would remain unnoticed.

But God does not ask the impossible from us. There was a large group of teenagers at the church, mostly living in the Hythe and Dibden Purlieu area of the Waterside. I found that I could relate to them, and they would talk to me. I grew to love this group of young people. On Sundays I would sit among them and worship with them. They would often visit me in Brockenhurst.

For my 50th birthday they bought me an address book in which they had written their names, addresses and phone numbers – sometimes more than once, for example Les Carr, not only appeared twice under C but also under L, S, and M. (Sir Les Carr, Mr. Les Carr, etc!) They became my Christian family, and were a great comfort to me.

However I decided not to obey God's word to me for a while – surely it would be alright if I waited until August or September – after Sally's wedding and John's retirement?

It was Friday, April 31st, the Summer term at Brocken-hurst, and the end of a busy week of teaching. I started to feel very ill. By lunchtime I knew I wouldn't make it through the afternoon, and that I had to go home. I had no idea what was the matter with me. I ached all over, felt very weak, and had stomach pains. I went to bed hoping that sleep was all I needed. I slept fitfully, and had violent dreams.

At 5 a.m. on Saturday, May 1st I got up, wrapped myself in a blanket, and sat in the rocking-chair by the gas fire in my study. Why did I feel so terrible? I cried out to God to help me.

'Why am I so ill? Please take this illness away.' I was shocked by His reply – He said that it wasn't His will that I should be ill. My illness was caused by my disobedience to His word to me to leave St. John's, and join the Community Church! As soon as I was prepared to obey Him, the sickness would go, and my peace and joy would be restored!

'But Lord, what about my daughter's wedding?' I said.

'You cannot want the most beautiful day of her life to be ruined? How could I do such a thing to her?' God replied, 'Who is more important to you, Me or your daughter?'

What could I say? I had promised to put God before everything else in my life. I would have to obey, and leave the church I had been part of for 18 years, less than three months before my daughter's wedding. Sally would be upset and my friends in the choir would be hurt. How could they ever understand?

At 9 a.m. I phoned Ken Ford, who was the leader of the Totton group of the Southampton Community Church, and asked if he could come and see me straight away; it was urgent.

'Well,' Ken replied, 'It would be easier if you visited us.'

'No, I am too ill to drive my car,' I said.

Ken consulted his wife Heather.

'Yes, we could come over in the afternoon.'

Thankfully I put down the receiver – I wouldn't have to wait too long.

May and Florence visited me during the morning, and could see the state I was in – hardly able to drag myself around. They were loving and concerned, fussing round me with cups of tea, etc. Florence lived alone nearby, a sprightly and petite widow in her 70's. I was always calling to see her, and loved her dearly. She was unhappy at the thought of my involvement with the Community Church, fearing it would take me away from her.

Ken and Heather eventually arrived with their two sons. We chatted together, and Ken played football in the garden with the boys. I was trembling and tearful as I explained what God had said to me. I asked to become a committed member of the church immediately. They were kind and cheerful about the whole thing, but very casual. Not even a prayer was said! I don't know what I had expected – Ken laying hands on me, and the illness suddenly leaving? Some deep ministry from them both, of prayer and acceptance? No, it couldn't have been more ordinary. Ken seemed more interested in playing football with his sons!

We had some tea together, and they cheerfully departed after an hour or two. But wow! As they went out of the door and got into their car, the illness and pain suddenly went. I was well again. I had been obedient. A deep peace came into my heart.

I checked back with the word God had given me – 'speak to Ken and Tony.' I hadn't yet spoken to Tony Hodder. He was the leader of the housegroup I had been visiting. I would phone him. I dialled his number, and as the phone rang in his house, I was overwhelmed with joy – it just bubbled up from inside. When Tony answered the phone I could hardly speak for the laughter in my voice. Fortunately he seemed to understand my incoherent message. 'Tony, I am joining the Community Church from today.'

I then went to tell Florence and May, I felt so well and happy. They were amazed at my transformation – the person incapable of dragging herself from a chair that morning, was now dancing up the road, laughing with joy.

At 10 o'clock that night, I wrote a poem to express my gratitude to God, for showing me so clearly His will for my life.

> *'We know that we have come to know him if we obey his commands.'*
>
> (1 John 2: 3)

> *'Jesus replied, "If anyone loves me, he will obey my teaching. My Father will love him, and we will come to him and make our home with him.'*
>
> (John 14: 23)

> *'but whoever listens to me will live in safety and be at ease, without fear of harm.'*
>
> (Proverbs 1: 33)

13

My New Family

On May 1st 1982 (the day I joined the Community Church) the E.D.W.J. notes were based on Acts 2 verses 42–47. *'The fellowship of the believers.'*

'They devoted themselves to the apostles' teaching and to the fellowship, to the breaking of bread and to prayer.'
'All the believers were together and had everything in common. Selling their possessions and goods, they gave to anyone as he had need. Every day they continued to meet together in the temple courts. They broke bread in their homes and ate together with glad and sincere hearts.'

This confirmed to me that God wanted me to be with Christians who devoted themselves to the apostles' teaching, to fellowship, to breaking of bread, and to prayer. Certainly the teaching, fellowship and prayer were all deeper and more important in my new family. The only thing we were more devoted to in St. John's was to the breaking of bread.

How I would miss those early mornings, up with the sunrise, going to church with the song of the birds, and the hush of the morning, to meet with Jesus.

I remember the first Easter after I became 'born again'. The Good Friday had been a day when I became speechless with the knowledge of what Jesus had done for me. I could neither eat, drink or talk. But at 3 pm as I stood in Boldre Church, the final words of Jesus were said, *'It is finished'*, (John 19:30).

I knew that it was finished. I knew that Jesus had

overcome all the powers of darkness including my sin, for ever. It was mind blowing. I went home with a thankful heart. I could speak again and could eat the hot cross buns with my family that had been bought specially for the day.

Good Friday

God gave His body on a tree for me,
The only Son of God was He,
Yet lovingly
He gave Himself, for me.

Torn, like a carcass, dripping there,
What can I feel of earthly care
or earthly need,
If He, did this, for me?

God gave His blood, upon a tree, for me,
So warm and red, it trickled down,
Over His face, from piercing crown,
Reddening the wood for me.

By this red wood,
By this torn flesh,
He conquered all my sin,
He vanquished death.

All praise, All thanks,
All glory, and all power
are His and only His,
Who died for me, in agony,
upon a tree.

On Easter day, I rose early. It was as if the whole world had been reborn. There was such joy in my heart that I wanted to dance and sing all the way to church. I had never felt like this before.

As I stood looking towards the altar at the silver chalice containing the wine – Jesus' blood shed for me – I saw a light shining out from the chalice all round. It was beautiful – the most precious offering that anyone could ever receive. God was showing me its holiness and power.

Easter Day

He is risen, Jesus lives,
Every sin on earth forgives,
Risen too, we bow before –
Him whom heaven and earth adore.

Death is conquered, man is won,
for our Father's heavenly home,
Victory is His today,
devils tremble, slink away,
knowing that their time has come,
for banishment to hell alone.

Joy and suffering are one,
In the heart of God alone,
Is this mystery revealed,
As the tomb has been unsealed,
So we see God's love.

Sharing every step we take,
weeping, laughing, He is there,
every pain, and joy to share,
Everywhere.

Risen Lord,
We bow before,
Thee, whom Heaven
and earth adore.

Could I get used to the different approach in the Community Church? Certainly we broke bread together as a real family, not only on Sundays, but sometimes during the week in our homes. Our hearts were glad, and we were sincere. What had been a very private and individual meeting with God in the Anglican Church, was now a family affair, where we prayed for each other and our needs. But it was only about once a month, and preparation was brief; I often felt unready.

I took to breaking bread alone when God woke me early, first making sure that it was what He wanted. I would lay the bread on a beautiful plate, put the wine in a lovely glass, arrange flowers, placing it all on a clean embroidered cloth. I would slowly prepare my heart and mind to commune with Jesus. He would often speak to me and strengthen me at these times.

My new Christian family believed in spending time together – they were 'devoted to fellowship'.

I soon learnt how much this fellowship meant to me. Three months after I joined the Community Church, I went on holiday to Italy. The trip had been planned early in the year. Sadly I would miss the Bible Week, when my new family would all be camping together in the New Forest.

On the night of August 11th 1982, I was in Umbria, half way between Florence and Rome. It was a Saturday and the first night of the Bible week. I suddenly felt sad and lonely. My new Christian family were together, worshipping and hearing from God, and I wanted to be with them.

I walked out into the hills near the villa. There was no one about. Perhaps watching a beautiful sunset would comfort me? The sunset was glorious, but my heart was still heavy. I started to weep.

'Why was I here, so far away from them all? What use was all this beauty if I couldn't share it with my Christian family?' I cried for a while, then realised that I was indulging in self-pity.

I had read a book, 'Prison to Praise'. If I praised God in my sadness, as the book suggested, perhaps the loneliness would go? So, through my tears, I started to praise and thank God for being where I was, and for the beauty around me. I kept going – my voice was saying the words, but my heart was still heavy.

Then, after about ten minutes, joy started to come into my heart. The words of praise became real, I really was thankful, and joyful too. I started to dance and sing, as the sun slowly sank below the hills on the far horizon, and the sky became a brilliant fire of colour.

It must have been a strange sight, a solitary English woman, shouting, singing, and dancing for joy, as the sun set over the hills of Italy. But I knew that even though we were many miles apart, I was one in heart and mind with my Christian brothers and sisters. We were worshipping God together.

'. . . . *Sing and make music in your heart to the Lord, always giving thanks to God the Father for everything, in the name of our Lord Jesus Christ.'*

(Ephesians 5: 19, 20)

When I returned from Italy, how wonderful it was to see everyone, and to catch up on all the news. I could again enjoy the many social gatherings which often had an International cuisine. I tasted some delicious new foods. Cakes made by Katrina, a Swiss lady, were mouthwatering! There were American cookies from Kimberly, who came from California, and Chinese food from Jenny who was Malaysian.

The ability to cook flans seemed to be a necessary part of the Church fellowship! So I bought some flan dishes, and my daughter gave me some help with the cooking. We were often having American suppers. As a busy career woman, I would usually be asked to bring the salads which were quicker to prepare.

14

Spiritual Battles

I love to spend time in prayer, and many of my new family were also 'devoted to prayer'. Joan and Tony were an older couple who had joined the church when I had. Like me they lived a long way from Totton. John and Janet were then living at Netley Marsh. These were my nearest church friends. I was a 'halfway house' in Brockenhurst, so we started to meet on Friday or Saturday evenings for prayer at my home.

How I looked forward to those times. I had a lovely Purbeck stone fireplace in my small lounge. I would light a log fire, get out my best coffee cups, and have the house ready and welcoming for their arrival.

Prayer in public never seems to come easily to me. God only gives me the first few words, so I must open my mouth and let Him do the rest. At first I found this was hard, but I gradually learnt that I could rely on God, He would never let me down, and anyway, I was prepared to be a fool for Christ.

Yet for many years, I had a secret ministry of prayer. I had shared this with no-one, and had no idea if anyone else in the world prayed as I did. It was a completely private affair between me and God.

When I offered myself totally to God in 1964, I saw Jesus' suffering and death on the cross as the way in which the powers of evil had been overcome. He was my model, and He had asked me to take up my cross and follow Him. I offered myself to God for suffering, and I didn't mind what that involved. I was prepared to do anything now that my life belonged to Him. It seemed to me that any form of human suffering, if borne willingly, overcame the forces of evil in the world.

I didn't know what to expect, but God gave me a gift of intercession. I would lie down to sleep at night, and would find my heart beating rapidly. As I went over in my mind the people I had recently been involved with, the beating would increase at a particular name. I then knew there was a battle to be fought for that person.

These battles took place over three days and nights. The first night I would pray constantly for about two hours until peace came, and the second night was the same. The third night I would sleep until between 3–5 a.m. and then I would battle until about 7 a.m. On the afternoon of the third day, there would be a final awareness that the victory was won.

There was always great joy in my heart that God used me in this way. Sometimes God allowed me to know what my prayer had achieved, at other times I didn't find out, but that wasn't important.

Only once did I want to opt out of the task. I was visiting friends, and had taken Sally and Stephen with me. A really powerful battle started to rage for the husband of my friend. On the first night I could hear the scream and roar of cars (he drove very fast). On the second night the cries and howls of animals in pain (he had been cruel to animals, and still beat his dog on occasions).

The day following I wanted to go home. The battles had been terrifying, and I hadn't dared to make a noise or switch on a light, as I was sleeping in a room with my children. At times I had hardly been able to breathe, and the effort was so intense that the sweat poured from me. The awareness of so much evil was almost unbearable.

I went for a walk, begging God to let me off another night of this torment. But I remembered what Jesus had done for me, and my promise to suffer for Him. I knew I must go on with the battle. The early morning session was terrible in its intensity, but God helped me to get through it. When I got up, I was able to respond cheerfully to my friends, and act as if nothing was wrong, and as if I had had a good night's sleep.

That afternoon I took the children and my friend's dog for a walk in a nearby park. At about 4 pm. the dog started to circle round me and then whined and barked, and came up to lick and nuzzle me. I knew that the battle was over, and that this beautiful and intelligent dog would never be beaten again, because his master had finally been released from a satanic spiritual oppression.

The battles were often different in the type of intercession required. Apart from keeping up a constant barrage of prayer, (at that time I could not speak in tongues, so I would repeat over and over again – 'In the name of the Father, the Son, and the Holy Spirit,' or 'Jesus, Jesus, Jesus,' or recite the Lord's prayer.)

I would sometimes groan or sob, or my whole body would, as it were, squeeze upwards. It was as if I was physically removing an evil force from the person I was praying for. If I was on my knees, I would push against the floor or wall with my hands, rather like childbirth in reverse. Occasionally the physical exhaustion I felt was great and I would need to lie down for a while afterwards to recover my strength. God never allowed these battles to occur when I was with other people. His timing was impeccable – the battle would just be over, and in would come one of my family or friends, etc.

I also prayed for people whom I had never met, and would never know. One night I woke and knew God was calling me to pray. Who was it? I started to go through names in my mind, but then I saw a picture. A man was lying in a prison cell, and standing over him were his tormentors. I particularly remember the hardened face of a large woman in a grey uniform. The man was being tortured for his faith. I sensed that he was somewhere in Russia. I started to pray for him. What he was enduring was terrible. For twenty minutes the battle raged, and I was weeping for him. Then I got angry – how dared they hurt this man of God! I started to shout at Satan to leave him alone in the name of Jesus. My anger and commands in Jesus' name were effective – his tormentors left him. There was such a sense of relief. I prayed for him to be healed of the pain he was in, and to know God's peace over him.

How glad I was that God allowed me the privilege of sharing His sufferings. If a few weeks went by without a battle, I felt sad and unused. However much sleep I lost, I always felt refreshed the next day, with a deep joy in my heart.

Just before I joined the Community Church, I read another book by Arthur Wallis entitled 'Pray in the Spirit'. I was so excited by what I read. Arthur described the sort of intercession that I had been secretly involved in for 18 years. I wasn't on my own after all! There were other people who 'agonised' in prayer as I did.

It was opportune that I read this book when I did, because God said I was to tell Ken and Heather of my intercessory work when I joined the Church. Without Arthur's book to refer to, I wouldn't have had the courage to do this.

I don't know what they thought of my confession, but it was a relief to know that I could share all of my heart with them. I didn't know why God wanted them to know all this, as I still believed that this type of prayer could only occur in private.

In November of that year I was with a prayer group in the Waterside area of the church. We were all sitting in a circle. Then the shock occurred – a 'travail of the soul' was starting within me.

'Lord,' I cried silently, 'I can't agonise here. They won't understand. They'll be upset, so please stop it.' I suffocated the groans and my desire to weep and kneel down, and hoped no-one had noticed. After the meeting, I decided that I could not be part of any more prayer groups. It would be too embarrassing for me and everyone else. I rang Ken, and explained my predicament.

To my horror and surprise, Ken firmly replied that I

was to explain what happened to me during intercession at the next prayer group, and I was to allow God to use me in this way when I prayed with other people!

Did he really understand what he was suggesting? I was only just getting to know the people in this church and I didn't want to be labelled as an oddity right from the start! I must ask God to guide me.

It was November 28th 1982 and God spoke to me. He said that He wanted me to obey Ken. Alone I had done much, but with others, even more would be accomplished. He was raising up men and women to stand against evil, and there were many battles to fight.

At the next meeting, I tried to explain to the group. The room was full of people from the church, most of whom I hardly knew. My voice trembled as I spoke. I didn't know if anyone would understand or even accept what I was saying. But Janet spoke to me afterwards. She did not dismiss my testimony. She said that she wanted to be used more effectively in intercession, and was prepared to battle with me. How grateful I was for her openness – it would be exciting to have the support of other Christians in this work.

When John and Janet came to pray at the weekends, they were not disturbed if I wept or groaned, and they both played an equally important part in the battles. Janet would get 'pictures' of what was happening, and physical sensations. John would take authority in Jesus' name. I was amazed to find that what had taken me several hours on my own, could now be accomplished in less than half an hour. No wonder God had said that more would be accomplished when I prayed with others.

However, it wasn't all serious and intense – we always had the joy and laughter of the battle won. I remember a couple of times, when Janet and I were on our knees, really getting into the battle, then we realised that John had happily dozed off on the couch. We collapsed in giggles, and prayed quietly until John was roused by a log falling in the fire, or was woken up naturally.

There was joy too in hearing the voice of authority. We had an American in the church for a couple of years. His name was John Babcock. I only had the pleasure of praying with him a few times, but how I enjoyed it! He always sounded like a cowboy riding along with all guns firing – it was more fun than watching a Western movie. I would laugh with the sheer joy of knowing that demons were on the run.

Yes, there are many battles to fight. God is raising up an army of men and women to fight against evil. These initial skirmishes are now turning into major warfare. My training for prayer warfare had been on an individual basis with God. I would soon find myself leading others through the rudiments of spiritual warfare, as God introduced me to Christians who were potentially gifted in this area of work. I was able to teach them by example and encouragement, to take their stand against the devil's schemes, and against spiritual forces of evil in the heavenly realms. Exciting times were ahead!

> *'Put on the full armour of God so that you can take your stand against the devil's schemes. For our struggle is not against flesh and blood, but against the rulers, against the authorities, against the powers of this dark world and against the spiritual forces of evil in the heavenly realms.'*
>
> (Ephesians 6: 11, 12)

> *'. . . . We do not know what we ought to pray, but the Spirit himself intercedes for us with groans that words cannot express.'*
>
> (Romans 8: 26)

In May 1982, I had no role in my new church, and I missed the work I had done in the choir at St. John's. Three weeks after joining I was given a 'word' from John Mason. It was at one of the housegroup meetings. I was chatting to John over coffee, and must have mentioned to him that I didn't know what God wanted me to do in the Community Church. I wrote down John's answer.

'I was to be like a new born lamb, and allow myself to be loved and cared for by the church. I was to learn from the elders. I was not to worry about having a specific job. I was to unlearn my past habits'.

I knew God had spoken to me through John. I would relax, and be loved and cared for, and learn all I could. I wondered what the past habits were that I must lose?

15

Changing and Learning

1. My relationship with the Church

My past habits didn't take long to start surfacing! On June 15th the church had a meeting at the Guildhall in Southampton. I sat in the middle of a row near the front, among all my young friends. The elders of the church were on the platform with the musicians.

I had begun to realise that I was afraid of becoming deeply involved with this church. It had been easy in the Anglican Church to keep my thoughts to myself. I was good at being bright and cheerful; whatever was going on in my heart and mind no-one needed to know. But here it was different; we were to speak the truth to each other in love. If I was feeling unhappy, depressed, worried, ill, etc., I shouldn't pretend anymore. Could I really trust myself to these Christians? I could trust myself to God, to Jesus, and the Holy Spirit, but other people might let me down.

At the end of the meeting there was a call for anyone with any fears to go forward for prayer. Absolutely no-one moved as we all stood in silence. I knew I needed prayer, but it was for the very thing that was holding me in my place. Why didn't anyone else go out to the front?

Then I found myself pushing past the others to get out of the row. I got to the gangway and stood there, alone. Ken had left the platform, and was standing in front of it. I looked desperately towards him. My legs had moved me into the aisle, but my head was telling me to go back!

Ken saw me, and, as he looked at me, I saw the eyes of Jesus, shining from His face – the love radiating out was overpowering. I was drawn forward as if to a magnet. I confessed my fear and self-consciousness, and Ken prayed for me to be set free. As he prayed, I began to feel totally accepted, not only by Jesus, but by those in whom Jesus lived, my covenant brothers and sisters in the church. I would be free to share my whole life and heart with them.

'. . . . speaking the truth in love, we will in all things grow up into him who is the Head, that is, Christ.'

(Ephesians 4: 15)

2. My relationship with God

One evening, Julie and Paul, two of my young friends in Totton, called to see me. We began to discuss the Holy Spirit. I confessed that although I had received the 'baptism of the Holy Spirit', I still couldn't relate to the Holy Spirit as a person. I had understood that He was the third person of the Trinity, but had little idea as to what that meant.

I seemed to be in the same position with the Holy Spirit that I had been in with Jesus before I became 'born again'. That is, I was glad Jesus loved me, and died for me, but I had no relationship with Him. This all changed when I asked Jesus into my life – He became a real person. I could relate to Him, and talk to Him. I knew He was with me.

Why hadn't the same thing happened for the Holy Spirit? Was it because my mind was filled with pictures of the Holy Spirit as a fire, a wind, or a dove? Even the name was hard to relate to. I could understand Father – I knew what a loving earthly Father was like. Jesus too; I had experienced friendship, and I could imagine Him as I read the stories of His life. He was my friend. But the Holy Spirit, or Holy Ghost – a spirit or ghost was not a real person, but something unreal and ethereal, that floated invisibly about. How could He be a person?

We prayed together, and Paul had a vision. He said that he saw three splendid and wonderful people in gorgeous robes, radiant with glory, standing in front of him. Two of them were upright and joyful, as they received love, honour, and worship. The third person was sad and thin, and bent over. No-one, it seemed, loved, honoured or worshipped Him.

We thought about the vision, and realised that the first two people were Father, and Jesus, and the third, sadly neglected person, was the Holy Spirit.

Oh dear, I was guilty. I knew that I did not love the Holy Spirit, and was causing His sadness and neglect. What could I do? If only He had a different name. I couldn't talk to 'Holy Spirit', we always said 'the Holy Spirit'. We didn't say the Jesus or the God. Why did we always put 'the' in front of His name?

I realised also that I acted and spoke as if He wasn't there, or couldn't hear me. I would say 'Dear Jesus, please send Your Holy Spirit to help me'. God showed me that this was rather rude. How would I like it if I was sitting in a room with friends, and was talked about as if I wasn't there? I imagined the conversation, 'Janet, could you ask Cynthia if she would like some tea?' Even though I am in the room, I am ignored.

I remembered that this can happen to handicapped people. Isabelle, a student who lived near me in Brockenhurst brought a friend to see me. Her friend was handicapped and in a wheelchair. I started talking to Isabelle, asking questions about her friend as if she wasn't there! I had assumed that someone in a wheelchair couldn't hear or speak!

How often parents discuss their children when they are present, or answer for them when they are questioned. Neither handicapped people nor children should be treated in this way, nor should Holy Spirit. God reminded me that Holy Spirit was always present with me, and I should talk to Him directly. He was the Comforter, bringing us wisdom, understanding, love, joy, and peace.

I tried calling Him Comforter – 'dear Comforter'. After all, I could think of some very comforting people. Then I tried to imagine this resplendent being standing by Jesus and Father. I still didn't seem to be getting very far; my old conditioning was a real barrier.

Next morning, driving to College, I thought that even if I didn't feel any love for Holy Spirit, I would decide to love Him. After all I wanted to love Him; I couldn't bear to think of Him all sad and unloved. He was also one with Jesus and Father, so they must be unhappy over my neglect of Holy Spirit.

I decided to declare out loud that I loved Him. 'I love You, Holy Spirit, I love You, Holy Spirit'. Driving along I kept this up for several miles, though the words seemed empty. Then amazingly, an incredible love for the Holy Spirit rose up within me. I felt an overwhelming and passionate love for Him. I really meant what I was saying. I had fallen in love with the Holy Spirit!

What joy; at last He was a person that I could love. He was real to me in a way that He had never been before. His happiness and joy at my love became my happiness and joy. It was wonderful.

How it hurt after that to hear people referring to the Holy Spirit as if He wasn't there. I realised how often we neglect to declare our love for Him, and to worship Him. There was a song that we sometimes sang – 'Father, I love You, I worship and adore You, Glorify Your name in all the earth'. These lines were repeated using 'Jesus, I love You', then 'Spirit, I love You, I worship and adore You'. I adored the Holy Spirit, I could worship and love Him. I was beginning to understand the Trinity at last.

No wonder St. Patrick had succeeded in Ireland where other Christians had failed. His hymn, 'I bind unto myself today the strong name of the Trinity', is known as St. Patrick's breastplate. That breastplate was Father, Son and Holy Spirit. Nothing could stand against the three in one and one in three, that St. Patrick carried before him into that land.

It was a few years later on March 5th 1980 that I became more deeply aware of the presence of the Holy Spirit. I love to dance, and some of the music of Vaughan Williams, Brahms, Vivaldi, other classical composers, and my Christian tapes, always get me to my feet.

That evening I was dancing in my lounge, sensing that Jesus was dancing with me. I was filled with happiness, and love for Him. When I stopped, a little breathless, I was aware of a gentle and beautiful presence standing beside me. I dared not turn my head to the right; I knew that a being of exquisite, shimmering beauty was standing there.

The moment was so fragile, and so precious. I held my breath, not daring to move. I was filled with awe at the holiness, gentleness, and beauty of this person – the Holy Spirit. I felt a pure joy that He should show Himself to me.

The moment passed all too quickly. Later I realised how rarely I let go of everything, and wait quietly, to allow the presence of the Holy Spirit to become real to me. His voice and His presence can be known, when we are empty of all else.

It reminded me of my enjoyment of nature – of sitting quietly in the Forest, hoping to see deer, or other animals nearby. Then having a beautiful butterfly land beside me, and not daring to move, for fear it would fly away. It is as we sit quietly, filled with love and peace, that the Holy Spirit can come close to us.

'I will ask the Father, and he will give you another Counsellor to be with you for ever – the Spirit of truth. The world cannot accept him, because it neither sees him nor knows him. But you know him, for he lives with you and will be in you.'

(John 14: 16, 17)

I was now able to talk to the Holy Spirit, and to

know His presence with me. I needed His help and guidance in all that I was doing. As Jesus had said, '. . . . *the Holy Spirit,* . . . . *will teach you all things* . . . .' (John 14: 26).

This did not stop me from talking to my Father, and to Jesus. I was once asked who you should talk to when you talk to God. I find that I talk to all three, both separately and together. My Father brings me all the love and security of perfect parenting. I talk to Him in particular when I am walking in the countryside, gardening, looking at the stars, watching the dawn and sunsets. He is the creator, and I marvel and wonder at His handiwork, and praise and thank Him.

My everyday activities I bring to Jesus – we can chat about them, and He helps me with them. He is my earthly model; I often ask the question, 'What would Jesus say or do in this situation?' and I try to act accordingly.

The Holy Spirit opens my eyes to the truth of God's word to us in the Bible, and I constantly ask for His help and guidance during intercession, and counselling. I try to remember to pray in the Spirit, that is in tongues, every day, knowing that my human mind cannot understand or know the needs of the Spirit.

Remembering the sadness of the Holy Spirit in the vision of the three glorious beings, I try not to neglect any one of the three. It reminds me of my relationship with the young women in the Church that have been put into my care. It is easy to give my time and attention to the one or two whose needs are obvious. The others, who may be less forthcoming about their needs, may get neglected, but need an equal portion of my prayers and concern.

3. God's relationship with me

It had always seemed to me that the best way to pray was on my knees. In the Community Church we prayed sitting or standing, etc., but when praying alone I liked to revert to the Anglican tradition of getting onto my knees. At night it helped to keep me awake, and in the morning it focussed my attention. I could kneel to see the beauty of the dawn sky, and to worship God. I could acknowledge my helplessness and my need of His love and direction in my life.

So I was very upset when I developed knee trouble. My right knee became very swollen and painful, and it hurt to kneel down. I went to the doctor, who diagnosed housemaid's knee – or water on the knee. He told me to rest my knee, and not to put any pressure on it by kneeling down to do housework, gardening, etc. I hadn't the courage to tell him that I spent a lot of time on my knees in prayer!

What was I going to do? How could I enjoy prayer without kneeling down? It just wasn't the same when I was sitting or standing. Sadly I realised I must obey the doctor, but despite this, my knee was still swollen and painful three months later. I felt very frustrated; not only could I not kneel down to pray, I couldn't ride my bicycle, or dance.

Why wasn't my knee getting any better? People in the church had prayed over my knee, and I had prayed; it would be an easy matter for Jesus to heal me, why didn't He?

In desperation I cried out, 'Jesus, I want to kneel down to pray, why haven't You healed me?'

Jesus gave me a strange answer, 'Would you kneel down to talk to your husband?'

I tried to imagine my husband coming into the room, and going down on my knees to talk to him – he would think I was crazy!

'No, of course I wouldn't,' I replied.

'I am your husband,' Jesus said.

I couldn't believe my ears. Jesus wanted me to talk to Him as I would to my husband. I realised that a husband would be really irritated by his wife always kneeling down

102

when she spoke to him! I remembered that in biological terms, kneeling down is a type of 'appeasement behaviour' and is used in situations where you are trying to forestall the wrath and anger of another person. I was behaving as if Jesus was constantly likely to attack me, and needed appeasing! He was my friend, and I didn't need to kneel down to talk to Him. He preferred me to talk to Him in a more natural position – sitting, standing, walking about, etc..

I found the concept of Jesus as my husband a strange one, but I discovered that it was biblical. Isaiah 54: 5 says *'For your Maker is your husband . . . .'*

By now, my desire to go down on my knees had nearly gone. After three months, I was getting used to either sitting or standing to pray. Now that I knew that Jesus didn't want me to kneel, it didn't matter that my knee was painful. Not surprisingly, my knee improved rapidly, and I was glad to dance and bicycle again. Also to get into some of my low kitchen cupboards, which had been almost inaccessible with one leg bent and the other straight!

For a year or so I totally avoided kneeling to pray, but now I do kneel on special occasions, and in obedience to the Spirit's prompting. This is usually when the burden to intercede is great, or during worship, when I sense the overwhelming presence of God.

I began to realise that if Jesus was my husband, I could trust Him for all the practical problems in my life; the sort of things that men are often skilled in. If the fence fell down, or the front door jammed, or my electrical machines malfunctioned, I would ask Jesus to help me. He always did; usually someone would call to see me, unaware of my problem, then offer to put it right! I found too, that if I couldn't do up a back zip, or button, or a necklace, and prayed, the problem was immediately solved. I had already learnt if I lost something important, to ask Jesus for help. He would always show me where to look for it.

'In that day,' declares the Lord, *'you will call me "my*

103

husband"; you will no longer call me "my master". I will betroth you to me for ever; I will betroth you in righteousness and justice, in love and compassion.'

(Hosea 2: 16, 19)

4. God the Creator

My work as a Biology teacher was also being influenced by my new family. Two young people in the Church challenged my acceptance of evolution, and gave me some Christian literature to read on the subject.

I taught the theory of evolution as if it were completely proven, and was not theory but fact, though even before I became a Christian I had thought that a lot of manipulation had gone into the use of the apparent evidence. Now I was no longer totally prejudiced into believing that this was the only possible explanation.

I watched a T.V. programme on the evolution of man. Richard Leakey was showing the fossil remains that had been obtained from the Olduvai Gorge, and other places in Africa. These were claimed to be the proof that man had evolved from ape-like ancestors.

I was horrified – surely there was more evidence than that! It was unbelievably scanty, and to my eyes, very inadequate. Supposing, after all, God had created man separately from other animals? I knew now that He could do anything He wanted. Seen from a totally different perspective, i.e. that a God existed, who had limitless power to create anything He wanted, a lot of the 'evidence' for evolution became highly suspect.

But why had God allowed us to have all this apparent evidence? Why were animals of the different groups so similar? Why hadn't God made everything so different that we couldn't possibly mistake His hand in creation?

'Father,' I asked, 'please, tell me why.' God gave me a reply. He said, 'Think of the work of a great artist, or a great composer.' All right, I thought of Van Gogh and Beethoven. 'Would you recognise one of the artist's

104

paintings or the music of that composer?' Well yes, I would – I prided myself on recognising the work of quite a few artists and composers!

'It is the same with My creation, each part of which bears the mark of My hand.'

I began to understand; each Beethoven symphony had been created separately, and was distinctive, yet the style of Beethoven was immediately apparent in the music. The fact that every living thing had its genetic code in the same molecule, D.N.A, was because this was the mark of God's hand. He had made this molecule and had used it to become the blueprint for each living thing.

The extraordinary thing was the limitless variety which could be achieved in this way. No two living things are ever the same (apart from identical twins). Man was indeed made in the image of his Creator, his creative efforts echoing the creative touch of God.

I watched another 'Horizon' programme on T.V. and saw the embryos of the different Vertebrate groups – apparently so similar in the early stages of growth. Yes, I began to understand. Here was the mark of God's hand.

Then, for the first time, I saw something I had often taught from slides and models. It was time-lapse photography of a developing embryo. I gasped at the wonder and beauty of the moving patterns of the cells; each cell knowing its appointed place, Gastrulation as the cells flowed inwards, the formation of the neural tube, as the cells flowed up in two waves along the embryo's back and joined together. It was as if an invisible hand was at work. God was indeed the master artist of creation, through whom, and in whom, everything has its being.

I wished that I could rewrite all the biology textbooks from this new viewpoint, to remove the basic lie of the evolutionary theory, that everything exists as a result of pure chance.

'For you created my inmost being; you knit me together

105

in my mother's womb. I praise you because I am
fearfully and wonderfully made;'

(Psalm 139: 13, 14)

5. The Lord's Glory

In early March 1989, we had a church leader's weekend in
Bournemouth. Tony Morton spoke on the first evening,
about the need for love, sacrifice and transparency among
us.

I woke at 3.30 a.m. on Saturday March 4th, and
meditated on the notes I had written down from Tony's
talk. Could we love each other as Tony had suggested
we should? Were we prepared to make sacrifices for
each other? We all like to keep areas of our thoughts
to ourselves. Could we be completely transparent with
other Christians?

How could we change? Perhaps if we had a greater
vision of Jesus and His glory, we would be more prepared
to abandon ourselves to each other? I thought about the
words of Jesus in John 17: 22.

'*I have given them the glory that you gave me, that they may
be one as we are one.*' What was this glory that would make
us one? I asked Jesus to show me His Glory (sometime
during that day), so that I could draw closer to Him and
to my brothers and sisters in the church. I then went back
to bed for a little more sleep.

I was excited when I woke again, and thought about my
request. Would I see Jesus' glory in a beautiful sunset, or
would it be during the worship that I would be aware of
His glorious presence? I was sure that my prayer could
be answered.

The morning meeting was good, and inspiring, but not
especially glorious, the afternoon meeting was similar,
and the sunset was not spectacular.

By the evening meeting I had forgotten my prayer. My
mind was filled with the enjoyment of the teaching and
fellowship we had received.

We met again in the Pavilion ballroom. This time it was dark outside, as we all stood to worship God. Then I started to feel strange – unable to worship. John Mason – standing beside me – was completely lost in adoration. What was the matter with me? I was feeling really unhappy. I stopped trying to sing, and sat down. A tremendous sadness began to fill me, and I started to feel pain in my hands and in my heart.

Then, in front of me, I saw a vision of Jesus on the cross, His body broken in love for everyone. I realised that I was being allowed to share a tiny part of His pain and suffering.

'Why are You reminding me of the terrible pain You endured Jesus?' I asked. 'Why now, Lord?'

Jesus replied, 'You asked to see My Glory. That is what I am showing you, the Glory of My love.'

I couldn't believe it! It wasn't what I had been expecting. I had thought that I might have a beautiful and ecstatic awareness of Jesus in majesty, not a revelation of His agonising death on the cross.

What could be glorious about unjustly endured suffering? The total humiliation, the jeering and sneers, the taunt, 'You saved others, but You can't save yourself!', the mocking and the insults. The whole thing was so ugly. I could only see the pain and the defeat. But Jesus was saying, 'Look at the Glory of My Love; this is where it was most clearly revealed.'

I began to understand that the love and forgiveness Jesus showed on the cross, despite His unjust and terrible suffering, was His greatest glory. He never once showed anger, hatred, or bitterness for His tormentors.

He was saying, 'Can you love in this way, with total sacrifice, total giving, nothing held back, even when you face undeserved pain and suffering?'

Romans 8: 17 says, '. . . . *we are . . . . co-heirs with Christ, if indeed we share in his sufferings in order that we may also share in his glory.*'

Somehow my vision was beginning to make sense. I

remembered some years before, grieving over a mongol boy and his family. They were godly Christians, so why had this son been born with such a handicap? God told me that the boy and his family were especially chosen to bear this pain. It was an honour, and a mark of His favour. In His kingdom, the boy would shine like a star.

Those who innocently suffer in their bodies, or in any other way, share the sufferings of Christ. When the pain and suffering is borne without anger and bitterness, it becomes transformed into glory.

None of us wants to suffer. Our human reasoning cries out for the abolition of all human suffering. Jesus went about relieving suffering, even though that suffering was brought into the world by man himself. It is man's disobedience to God that constantly gives Satan the power to attack both the guilty and the innocent.

Suffering isn't what Father wants for His children. He didn't want it for His own Son, but we cannot avoid the consequences of our fallen nature. Satan, however, does not have the last word. When the innocent bear pain without bitterness and complaint, it becomes transformed into Glory, turning back the tide of evil.

Sometimes, pain and suffering is not just physical. It can be in the heart and mind; the sudden and inexplicable death of a loved one, the rejection by a husband, wife, children, or friend, etc.

Jesus' death shows us that the loneliness of loss and rejection is something He shares and understands. As we refuse to believe that Satan has the victory, and continue to believe in God's faithfulness to us, then '. . . . *weeping may remain for a night, but rejoicing comes in the morning*' (Psalm 30: 5).

With Job we can say, '*Though he slay me, yet will I hope in Him . . . .*' (Job 13: 15), knowing that our personal crucifixion of pain, will lead to the joy of a resurrection in our lives.

'*The Lord blessed the latter part of Job's life more than the first . . . .*' (Job 42: 12).

But how did all this relate to the Church? I had wanted to see Jesus' glory, to enable me to get closer to my Christian family. The verse from John 17 had implied that the glory of Jesus in us would make us one.

Perhaps God was saying that in our church family we must be prepared to face pain and misunderstanding, condemnation, or rejection, and like Jesus, say nothing, only showing love and forgiveness to our persecutors?

And that we should not try to get other Christians to agree with us, and take sides with us against our persecutors. Nor should we opt out, and go elsewhere, to another church group that might be more prepared to accept us, and agree with us.

We all need love and understanding, so the hardest battle of all is when our own families reject us. Is it possible to love those in our church family who do not understand or love us? Perhaps that victory of love and unity for the whole Church will only be achieved when self-righteousness, self-justification, and pride disappear?

Can we go on loving, and saying nothing to defend ourselves, when our most deeply held convictions are under attack, and when we receive unjust criticism for our behaviour?

This was Jesus' glory; could it be ours? The glory of His totally selfless love overcame the powers of death. We could share that glory, by accepting the painful and unjust criticisms of our fellow Christians without complaint.

Could we love all other Christians as Jesus loves them, totally and unconditionally? Was this the way in which the divisions and disunity between us all would be healed? Could we allow those irritations between us to be like the grain of sand in an oyster, enfolding the pain in gentleness and kindness, so that it could be transformed into that pearl of great price – the glorious and radiant Church for which Jesus laid down His life?

'How good and pleasant it is when brothers live together

*in unity! . . . For there the Lord bestows his blessing, even
life for evermore.'*

(Psalm 133: 1, 3)

'*. . . . But if you suffer for doing good and you endure
it, this is commendable before God. To this you were called,
because Christ suffered for you, leaving you an example, that
you should follow in his steps.'*

'*He committed no sin, and no deceit was found in his
mouth.' When they hurled their insults at him, he did not
retaliate; when he suffered, he made no threats. Instead, he
entrusted himself to him who judges justly.'*

(1 Peter 2: 20–23)

6. Mother – Father God

I was ill one Sunday, with mild 'flu, and couldn't get to
church. The message preached is always taped, so that
those unable to hear the word are not neglected.

Later that week I lay on my couch, and listened to the
Sunday message. It was from a young man called Tony
Rozée. He was talking about forgiveness. I realised that
I needed to forgive my mother (even though she was
dead and in Heaven) for her lack of physical affection
and approval for me when I was a child; for the times
when she told me that she had never wanted children.

It wasn't her fault; she did all she could to be a good
mother, but she had received very little affection herself
as a child. She had been put into an orphanage when her
father died suddenly, leaving her as one of the youngest
children in a large family with no means of support.

As I forgave her from my heart, I suddenly had a
huge longing for the comfort of a mother, which was
something I had never consciously needed before. But
I was living alone; who could bring me this comfort? I
cried out to God,

'Please Father, I need a mother to love me.' His reply
was, 'I am your mother.'

110

No! God was my Father. How could He be my mother? I didn't want Him to be my mother. My mother was always critical of my appearance, and intellectual ability, and despite my efforts to please her, was unable to speak out encouragement or pleasure at my achievements. What sort of mother would God be?

I discovered a verse in Isaiah which talked of God as Mother.

'*As a mother comforts her child, so will I comfort you*; . . . .'

(Isaiah 66: 13)

So it was true, God could bring me the comfort of a mother that I now needed. And Jesus said in Matthew 23: 37, about Jerusalem,

'. . . . *how often I have longed to gather your children together, as a hen gathers her chicks under her wings,* . . . .' which was a very maternal image.

One of the names of God in the Old Testament is El Shaddai, which can be translated as 'The breasted one'.

Perhaps we all need to learn to receive mother love and comfort from God, and to worship the qualities of Mother in God, as we already worship the qualities of Father.

Yes God was my Mother, as well as my Father. But I longed to experience that comforting love of a mother in reality. I thought of all the cuddly, plump women I knew – how wonderful to be comforted by one of them!

The next morning I was still hungry for mother love. At about 10 a.m. the front door bell rang. Kimberly and her son Aaron had come to visit me. I invited them in. Kimberly said, 'We have both come to give you something Cynthia. It's a big hug.'

Well, neither of them knew of my prayer. This must be from God. Kimberly gave me a wonderfully comforting hug, and I knelt down to receive the same from Aaron.

Now Kimberly happens to be the thinnest woman I know. She had anorexia as a young woman, and still

111

struggles to keep the right weight. She was definitely not one of the comforting motherly types that I had in mind! Neither was Aaron, who was a very masculine eight year old. But both of them had given me that deep motherly comfort that I now craved.

I realised that God was showing me something – I had a stereotyped image of 'mother'. It needed to be changed. The qualities of 'mother', like the qualities of 'father', could be contained in a male or a female, and were not dependent on age, sex or size! If this was true of us, then I could understand that it was true of God.

That day I went down to the photographers to buy some picture frames. They were giving away free clip-on animals if you bought two frames, so a small black and white panda was slipped into my bag. You can imagine my surprise when I took it out, and read what was on its red waistcoat – 'I want my Mummy'.

The little panda is now clipped to my driving mirror, as a daily reminder that (like a baby panda) I can cuddle up to the wonderful motherly comfort and security of my Father God.

7. God's final plan

I offer you the following thoughts, which came into my mind as I was meditating on the whole purpose of male and female in God's plan.

The Bible shows us that Jesus came from God, and is equal to God, being a unique expression of the Godhead. Jesus is the image of God.

'*He* (Jesus) *is the image of the invisible God, the first-born over all creation.*'

(Colossians 1: 15)

'*The Son is the radiance of God's glory and the exact representation of his being, sustaining all things by his powerful word . . . .*'

(Hebrews 1: 3)

112

In the same way, woman came from man.

> '*So the Lord God caused the man to fall into a deep sleep;
> and while he was sleeping, he took one of the man's ribs* (or
> part of the man's side) *. . . God made a woman from the
> rib* (or part) *he had taken out of the man, and he brought
> her to the man. The man said, 'This is now bone of my bones
> and flesh of my flesh;'*

> (Genesis 2: 21–23)

As Jesus is co-equal with God, so woman is co-equal
with man.

There are people who do not believe Jesus to be fully
part of God and co-equal with God. In the same way there
are those who do not see woman as co-equal with man.
Both fall into a similar deception.

As Jesus came from God, a poured-out expression of
God's self, so woman came from man, as a poured-out
expression of man. When men or women deny this, then
they deny and impoverish themselves.

Both man and woman are a reflection of God, being
made in the image of God, and will together become the
Bride, to fulfil the longing of Jesus, the Bridegroom.

> '*So God created man in his own image, in the image of
> God he created him; male and female he created them.*'

> (Genesis 1: 27)

The Bible talks of the Church as the Bride of Christ.
Jesus waits for the fulfilment of unity with the Bride, in
the way that an earthly bridegroom is fulfilled through
marriage.

As we are made in the image of God, one of the
qualities of God must be this longing for union in love
and marriage, which is reflected in the earthly love of
man and woman. All things will be completed when this
longing in God's heart is fulfilled at the marriage of Jesus
to His Bride, the Church.

'. . . . *Hallelujah! For our Lord God Almighty reigns. Let us rejoice and be glad and give him glory! For the wedding of the Lamb has come, and his bride has made herself ready.*'

(Revelation 19: 6–7)

As God contains male and female in His heart, it seems that a final unity of these two is His plan for us all. Having 'breathed out' these qualities of male and female, He intends to bring them back together in glorious fulfilling unity, for eternity.

So the expression of unity between man and woman in marriage is a forerunner of the unity which will one day exist in God's heart. This unity, of man and woman, results in joy for the bridegroom.

'. . . . *as a bridegroom rejoices over his bride, so will your God rejoice over you.*'

(Isaiah 62: 5)

We see in this joy a foreshadowing of the joy of God, when He shares the joy that Jesus will know through His marriage to His bride, the Church.

This joy already permeates the whole of God's creation. With water birds it is fascinating to see the dance of joy, which the male performs after mating. It seems to be an expression of pure delight.

As these thoughts came into my mind, I found them difficult to grasp, and yet in many ways so simple and obvious. In case I have not adequately explained, I offer a summary.

1. Jesus came from God, and is co-equal with God. Jesus has always existed in God, but was drawn out of God, to fulfil God's plans. Jesus is the image of God.
2. We are also needed, as part of the fulfilment of God's plan, and were made in the image of God. God is reflected in man and woman. We were drawn

114

from the dust, which forms the carbon-based molecules of our earthly bodies.

3. Woman was drawn out from man, as Jesus was drawn from God. As Jesus is co-equal with God, so woman is co-equal with man.

4. The union in marriage of man and woman is a partial forerunner of the union of the male-female qualities of God's heart.

5. God's longing for this union will be satisfied when the Bride (the Church) representing the qualities of God's female nature, is united with the Bridegroom – Jesus, who will represent the qualities of God's male nature.

6. What is earthly and of the dust cannot be united with what is heavenly. But, through receiving the blood-bought redemption of Jesus' sacrifice, our earthly bodies will be transformed into heavenly bodies.

7. So the Bride – the united body of believers, the Church, will be drawn back to God, through marriage with Jesus. This marriage will fulfil God's ultimate and eternal plan for unity which will realease endless joy.

8. This joy is already evident in the joy following the fulfilment of sexual unity. But, because of our fallen and sinful nature, this joy is rarely what it could be.

'. . . . we have been made holy through the sacrifice of the body of Jesus Christ once for all.'

(Hebrews 10: 10)

'For we know in part and we prophesy in part, but when perfection comes, the imperfect disappears. Now we see but a poor reflection; then we shall see face to face.'

(1 Corinthians 13: 9–12)

16

Moving House

It was Christmas Day 1982, and the Lord woke me early. I sat up in bed, and reached out for my 'Daily Light'. As I opened it to read the scriptures for the day, a voice spoke in my head.

'I want you to move to Southampton.'

'When Lord?' I asked.

'In the Spring,' He replied.

It was 6 a.m. – was this meant to be a Christmas present? Jesus was homeless on the day He was born, and now God was asking me to leave my home on Christmas Day!

I am a countrywoman at heart. Without being able to see the whole of the sky, to enjoy the sunrise and sunset, to see the stars and moon at night, I feel only half alive. I like to be able to walk out of my gate straight into lanes, fields and woods. I love to be among trees, by streams, and on heathland. Watching birds and other animals always brings me close to their Creator.

My large garden, full of flowers and well stocked with fruit and vegetables was a delight to me. In the Autumn I made jams, jellies, and pickles to fill the shelves of my walk-in larder.

Why Southampton? It was noisy and full of people, and traffic. Where could I find peace and solitude there? Perhaps God wanted me to be more involved with the young people I saw in Shirley on Saturday evenings?

I would drive over from Brockenhurst to help in the coffee-bar that the church ran for youngsters who were unemployed, or from broken homes. There was little for them to do in Shirley except wander the streets, or spend time in the amusement arcade.

Despite unemployment and little money, some of them had extraordinary hair-dos spending a lot of their time dying and spiking their hair into exotic colours and shapes. The boys were the most colourful. The girls mostly dressed in black, with thick make up and black hair.

Some Saturday evenings there would be aggression and trouble. We were often only a small group of about six adults, from a team of twelve. We met to pray during the week, and to arrange a programme of music, videos, etc . . .

I was allowed to start a bookstall, with as many give-away leaflets as possible. A table was set up outside the main hall in the entrance where it was quieter. The young-sters would gather round and chat, taking the free leaflets, and looking at the books. There were New Testaments to give to anyone who seemed really interested.

We all did what we could to show them that we cared for them, and to tell them about Jesus. Some of the team would go to the Amusement Arcade to invite the children back for coffee, and distribute leaflets on the street. We got to know the 'regulars', who came every week.

It was always a relief to drive back to the peace of Brockenhurst. Yet I knew it wasn't enough to talk to the youngsters, and give them one evening off the streets. Some of them needed accommodation and care during the week, and we weren't available.

Was God wanting me to move closer to them? Perhaps I was to buy a larger house where I could have some of the girls to stay? I asked for guidance, and God replied that He would lead me to the place He had prepared for me, and that I didn't need to plan or worry. I felt sure He must want me to move to Shirley.

I spoke to the Church elders, saying that I believed that God wanted me to move to Southampton. Dick suggested that I ask God for confirmation, so for three days I fasted and prayed.

I had been concerned about my mother. She lived with Josephine my younger sister, near Leicester, but since Jo's marriage things had been difficult. Jo was arranging for Mum to go into an old people's home. I knew she would be unhappy about this, so I had been wondering if she should come and live with me in Brockenhurst.

On Sunday January 2nd, 1983 my older sister Edwina phoned me. Mum had been allocated a self-contained ground floor flat in a group of flats for old people. It would be only a few miles from Jo's house, and Mum was really happy with the idea. One of my obstacles had gone, confirming that I would be free to move.

But what about my son Stephen? He was just 18, and when I told him that I was thinking of moving to Southampton, he was upset, and said that he wouldn't come with me. All his friends lived in the Lymington area which he loved, and he was working in Lymington. Like me he disliked towns and cities. He said that he would move in with his friends.

I knew that they drank, smoked, and experimented with drugs – they weren't Christians. How could I move if this drove him away from me? I talked to God about it, but He said to me, 'Who is more important to you, Me or your son?'

I didn't want to go to Southampton. I loved my Victorian house, and had spent many hours improving and decorating it, and making the garden beautiful.

I entered some weeks of darkness. I was already almost alone. I had given up the church I loved, my husband had left me. My daughter was married and living far away in Sheffield. Now I was being asked to give up my home and my son.

I knew that I must obey God, but the future stretched bleakly before me, with the last of my earthly joys removed. On January 31st I cried out to God. Why was He taking all I loved away from me, yet not showing me anything of the future? His reply included the following.

'It is in the dark that faith is tried and tested, it is in the dark that My love alone you will cling to. It is in the dark that you will most clearly feel My arms around you. For it is when you cannot know the warmth of human comfort, that you will reach out to be comforted by Me, and will grow in the knowledge of My love for you.'

He also showed me a picture of a bulb in a pot, which, like the hyacinths I planted every Autumn, had to be kept in the dark to encourage it to grow. Only when the shoot was well above the fibre could it come out into the light.

I was like the bulb. There were things that I could only learn in the dark, and a growth that could only take place in this time of uncertainty for my future. I must accept this time of emptiness and waiting, and allow God to come close to me through it.

On the first day of Spring (March 21st) I went to an estate agents, and put my house up for sale. I also started to look for a house in Shirley. But my church elders were trying to encourage me to buy a house in Totton, or the Waterside. When they suggested these other places, I felt upset and unhappy.

Eventually things came to a head. Dick rang me at College to suggest that I look at a house in Pooks Green, which is a few miles south of Totton. It was near his home.

Didn't he understand? I wanted to move close to my young friends in Shirley! Tearfully I put the receiver down. 'What is happening Father? You said the church would guide me, so why is Dick suggesting Pooks Green and not Shirley?'

After College I had a headache, and needed some fresh air. I drove out to an area of heathland for a walk. It was a grey day with an icy wind and driving rain. I only had a light mac on, and no hat, but I didn't care. I had to get this problem sorted out with God.

I started to walk across the heath. The icy rain stung my face, and mingled with my tears. I was unhappy, and unsure of the future. I cried out to God for help.

It was a wild and miserable day. There was no-one about to wonder what I was doing, fighting my way across the heath, shouting at God!

I got completely soaked, but somewhere on that walk I gave in, and stopped fighting. It really didn't matter where I went. Whatever God wanted, I wanted. I would lay down all my ideas, thoughts and plans and trust that God would lead me through my new church family. I suddenly felt at peace, my headache cleared, and, dripping wet, I returned to my car.

I had been blissfully unaware throughout all of this that I had been trying to manipulate the elders to my way of thinking. God had said that they would guide me, but I had been expecting them to guide me in the direction I wanted to take!

God knows our weaknesses. He knew that I couldn't contemplate a move to Southampton without some tangible goal. So He had allowed me my completely impractical dream of single-handedly taking on the young drop-outs of Shirley. Once this had ensured my obedience to move house, He began to gently ease me away from my dream to His real plan for me. There was no way that I could have faced the move I eventually made, without a complete breaking of my self-will.

At the next house group meeting, I talked of my uncertainty about my future home. John spoke to me.

'Cynthia, I think you should look in Totton.' Oh no! I was horrified. I knew God was speaking to me through John, but Totton seemed to me to be the most boring and unattractive place that I knew. My aim had always been to drive past, or through it, as quickly as possible. There was nothing that would induce me to move to Totton, except obedience to God.

Reluctantly I went to an estate agents in Totton. The few houses that were available in my price range were unsuitable for one reason or another. By now I had a definite buyer for my house in Brockenhurst. I must find another home soon.

The Totton estate agent that I was involved with was a forceful and determined young woman. There was a house for sale that I had flatly refused to inspect. On the outside I thought it looked like a prison. The front garden was just a tarmaced extension of the pavement, and apart from some variation in tiling and brickwork the front of the house was a blank and monotonous vista, of garage door, flat walls, and plain windows. The front door was tucked away at the side.

I could never live in a house like that! It was also on a busy road, and I hated the sound of constant traffic. However, the estate agent persuaded me to have a look at it. She told me that it was really nice inside! As she had worked hard to help me, I couldn't keep on refusing. So I made an appointment to view the property.

I arrived in Totton early, on the day I was to inspect the house, and parked my car to do some shopping. A lady in the church called Thelma Vallis cycled past me, and stopped for a chat. When I told her where I was going she asked if she could come too. I was pleased that I would have some company and another opinion, so Thelma left her bicycle, and got into my car.

As the estate agent had said, the house was much pleasanter inside than I had expected. It was only a year old. The small garden was laid out with a patio and lawn. Even so, I could not imagine myself living there – it was so modern.

There was central heating throughout, with a gas fire in the lounge. It had a tiny kitchen, with no larder, there were no wardrobes, and few cupboards. The lounge was north facing, with no sun. No, I didn't want this house.

We were standing in the lounge, and I was looking at the highly patterned carpet – not my taste at all – when to my amazement, Thelma started to bounce up and down with excitement.

121

'Cynthia, I know this is the house God wants you to have.' I was stunned – was this really where I was to live? But Thelma was a person I could trust – a woman of great love and humility, and very close to Jesus.

'All right Father. You said that You would guide me through the Church. I believe You are speaking to me through Thelma. I'll make an offer to buy this house.' Someone else had already made an offer; it seemed unlikely that I would be successful. But the other buyer could not sell her home, and eventually, after several crises, the contracts were signed.

I was to move to Totton on August 19th 1983. Edwina promised to come over for the day to help me, even though this was her birthday. Stephen said that he was going to move all his belongings to Lymington.

Two weeks before the move, I went to a Church Bible week at Shepton Mallet in Somerset, so there would be only one week when I returned home to sort out my camping gear, and finish packing. I hoped it would be enough time to do everything. I had already lightened the load of my material possessions, as God had asked me to. This was just as well, as there would be no greenhouse, garden shed or conservatory, and fewer cupboards.

The seven days before I moved were very hot, and I stood for hours filling packing cases. To my surprise, at the last minute, Stephen changed his mind about his possessions. He wanted them to be taken to Totton, only keeping a minimum back to take with him to Lymington.

By the time moving day arrived, I was exhausted, and my ankles had swollen up to twice their normal size. I locked my heavy front door with its lovely brass fittings, and climbed into my ancient Triumph Herald that was full of house plants. As I drove down the road I looked back, tears in my eyes.

'My lovely home Lord, I don't want to leave it.'

In Totton I no longer had a porch full of plants to welcome me, just a glass front door with a grey metal letter box. Sadly I unlocked the door and stepped over the threshold. Then, wham, a tremendous flood of joy enveloped me. I started to laugh – I was bubbling over with happiness – was this possible? How could I feel so joyful, when I didn't want to be here? I knew my joy must be from God. He was pleased with my obedience – I was where He wanted me to be, so my spirit was rejoicing.

For the next three days I was blissfully happy. I sat among the chaos (feet up because of my painful ankles) watching other people unpacking for me. My sister Edwina was wonderful on moving day; we managed to sort out all Stephen's possessions in the largest bedroom, so that if he ever returned, he would know that there was a room waiting for him.

It had been a long and painful effort getting to Totton, but, once I had arrived, my new family took over. Everyone came to help. Dick wired in my electric cooker, Jan, his wife, shortened my lounge curtains, Les sorted out my sound systems, etc. It was nearly a week before I could walk properly, and I couldn't find anything, but I felt at home.

I now had a long drive to work each day in my old and unreliable car. Having moved to a cheaper house, I had money to spare, so, for the first time in my life, I could afford a brand new car. I went from having the oldest car in the staff car park to the newest! I also discovered the bliss of an integral garage. The car was always warm and dry on the coldest morning. No more scraping ice from windows, or freeing frozen door locks to get to College.

Several weeks later, Stephen had a row with the friend he was staying with in Lymington, so he came back to stay in Totton. God had sent my son back to me!

As I look back over my seven years in Totton, I realise that there has been a constant stream of young people (mostly Christian) into my heart and home.

God needs those who will care for the young from every background. Sometimes those who seem well-equipped for life in the material sense, are in great need emotionally. So it was not to the young drop-outs of Shirley that I was called, but to the young people of Totton, who needed God's love and encouragement in their lives.

For me, these became my sons and daughters, sent by God to replace my earthly family, and to bring me much love, joy and companionship. For one young man in particular, God gave me a great love and compassion.

Andy's greatest need was for love and understanding. In April 1985, he went to a Church of England weekend for young people at Alresford house. There he knew a love that overwhelmed him. He came back sad at leaving this love behind.

He wanted to know what love was, and how we should love. I couldn't give him a satisfactory answer, but at 2a.m. the following morning I woke, and realised that although I couldn't explain love (as I couldn't explain God, and God is love) I could see the qualities of love. It was as if love was an invisible light. If a prism was placed in front of that light it would break up into a rainbow of colours. We were like prisms, and the smoother, and clearer we were, the more complete and beautiful the rainbow. I wrote the following to give to Andy.

What is love?

Love has many colours, and each one is beautiful. There is JOY, that pure opening delight of the heart, which comes from obedience, and is present when we are with those we love, and with God.

There is PEACE, that deep calmness and certainty that all is well whatever the circumstances.

There is SECURITY, the unshakeable awareness of

God's arms, around and below us, always holding us close to His heart, never failing us.
There is BEAUTY, that leaves you gasping, with its overwhelming impact, lifting your soul and spirit away from self, to unite you with itself.
There is TRUTH, that leads you into new dimensions, foreshadowing eternity.
There is HOLINESS, which prostrates you in awe and wonder before its blinding purity, slaying, then exalting you.

What is it to love?

It is to abandon ourselves to the beloved, to open our hearts, and to both give and receive joy in that abandonment.
It is to believe in the beloved, and to be believed, without doubt, or fear so that we can be enfolded in peace.
It is never to question the arms of love around us, and never to have our love questioned, for love never ends.
It is to open our eyes to drink in love's beauty, and to allow love to drink in all of ours.
It is to listen to, and follow the truth of love, and to only give of our truth to the beloved.
It is to die at the holiness of love's touch, and then to be united with the beloved, in an unknown and unbelievable ecstasy.

For those who love, know God.
The love that was crucified to give a crown,
and those who love, know the hand of God crucifying, and then crowning, breaking apart to rebuild, purifying to glorify.
And those who can abandon themselves for another, who can trust and believe with no falsehood, and who can die for love, will know the kingdom of

Heaven, in their hearts, and their homes. In their families and with their friends in this life, and the next, for ever.

'My command is this: Love each other as I have loved you. Greater love has no one than this, that one lay down his life for his friends.'

(John 15: 12, 13)

17

Healing the Broken Church, Past, Present and Future

1. The past

There have always been crises in the Church. Satan's activities are primarily focussed on disrupting and dividing the Church, trying to bring about its downfall. But God's purpose, to provide a bride for His Son Jesus, cannot be thwarted.

Early in the thirteenth century, the Church was in grave danger of collapse. But through God's call on the life of one young man, Francis Bernadone, this collapse was prevented.

Saint Francis of Assisi has always been a special hero of mine. He heard from God, and obeyed. In 1206, when he was twenty four years old, he gave up everything to follow Jesus. His life of riches, popularity and pleasure was left behind, as he embraced loneliness, poverty, and rejection. He became a beggar, without worldly comfort or fun, but with the deep joy that comes from obeying God.

He followed Jesus' commands literally. Jesus had said that we cannot be His disciples unless we give up everything to follow Him – home, family, possessions, friends. We were to take up our cross daily. We should give to anyone who asked for anything from us. If we were poor, meek, or persecuted, we would be blessed.

From Jesus' instructions, Saint Francis developed his life of humility, simplicity, poverty, and prayer. The friars who eventually joined him were to be humble and poor; happy to be identified with the outcasts, and the unloveable, glad to be despised, and patient in any trouble. Their 'perfect joy' would come from gladly and patiently bearing pain, insult and shame for the love of Christ, as did Francis. After his passionate love for God, and for mankind, he loved and respected all living things as being part of God's creation.

In the summer of 1982, I went with my friend Ann to her parents' holiday home in Italy. It was situated in the hills opposite Assisi and Perugia. I wanted to go to all the places that Saint Francis had walked, and, in my imagination, get close to this extraordinary man of God.

During that holiday I would get up before sunrise, and go out into the hills, taking a rug and my Bible, to spend time with God. I sat looking across the valley, and would watch the sun, rising behind the hills above Assisi, changing the quiet greyness to sparkling colour and light, with the birds singing their praises to God, and wild flowers, gently opening in the warmth of the sun.

I knew that I was where Saint Francis had been. These were the hills on which he had walked. The flowers and birds were the same ones that he had enjoyed. I drank in the peace and the beauty, and sat singing my praises to God with the birds. I felt very close to God, and to Saint Francis.

We went to Assisi, and visited the Basilica of Saint Francis; a strange double church on top of a church, with pink washed walls, and blue turrets. It was very hot, and it was a relief to go into the cool church, and look at the beautiful paintings by Giotto on the walls, especially the one of Pope Innocenzo III, dreaming of Francis supporting the falling Church on his shoulders. It was this dream that ensured that Francis was not turned away when he went to the Pope, asking to start his order of friars.

We visited the church of Saint Damien, just outside the walls of Assisi. It was very early in the morning on the last day of my holiday. We were going to have breakfast on the hills above Assisi, and watch the sunrise. We thought we would be too early for the church to be open, but no, early mass was in progress. In the front of the church stood the brown-robed Franciscans with their rope belts, singing in simple plainsong. Above their heads was the Byzantine cross with the painted figure of Christ on it.

It was here that Francis had knelt and asked for guidance, and heard the words, 'Francis, go and repair my Church, which, as you see, is falling down.' It was as if the figure on the cross was speaking to him.

For a few minutes we knelt in the doorway of Saint Damien, then we left, and drove up into the hills. There we saw a sunrise that was almost beyond description, breathtaking in its beauty. The rolling hills thrown into sharp relief – turquoise, green and gold. We sat and breakfasted, looking down on Assisi, shining like a white jewel in the early sunshine.

The meek Saint Francis did indeed prevent the Church from falling down, as hundreds and thousands of men and women turned from the materialism and selfishness of the time, to bring a new humility and caring love into the Church, throughout Christendom.

'Blessed are the meek, for they will inherit the earth.'

(Matthew 5: 5)

'. . . . if you want to be perfect, go, sell your possessions and give to the poor, and you will have treasure in heaven. Then come, follow me.'

(Matthew 19: 21)

2. The present

Healing of a different sort is needed today. The Church is not crumbling from rotten foundations, but is helpless in its broken and fragmented state. It isn't propping up that we need, as in the thirteenth century, but cementing together.

Many books have been written on the Ecumenical

movement, and many Christians have been actively working to bring healing to our divisions. How this should be tackled is a very big issue; it seems that several ways are needed, to bring together the broken parts of the Church.

I will describe one exciting example of the joining together of two denominations. It happened to involve my own family.

In 1984, my daughter Sally went to Sheffield for one of her occupational therapy placements. Her husband, John, was still in the South, training to be an accountant. They had no settled home, and Sally would soon be qualified and looking for a job. Where would they live?

Sally got to know a young man through the Sheffield hospital. He lived alone in a terraced house in Crookes, an area to the north west of Sheffield, and attended Saint Thomas' Church nearby. He invited Sally and John to share his home, and to look for employment in Sheffield.

John needed no second invitation – he had already left his accountancy training, as he wanted to work with computers, and was looking for a job. So he went to be with Sally in Sheffield. They started to attend Saint Thomas' Church, which was under the leadership of Robert Warren.

This Church of England had gone through a big upheaval. There had been a costly rebuilding programme, and later, union with the nearby Baptist Church. It seemed unbelievable! How could such a union be possible?

All the details of the way God moved to provide the money for rebuilding, and to bring about union, are well documented in Robert Warren's book 'In the Crucible'. It makes fascinating reading, but, as this wasn't published until 1989 I had no real idea as to how such a Church could function. It was a very new venture, and to ensure that the separate traditions of the two denominations would not be lost, rules had been carefully formulated.

Unfortunately, Sally and John came up against the rules for baptism. John hadn't been baptised as a child, and now that he had become a Christian, wanted to be baptised by total immersion. Sally had been both christened as an infant, and confirmed at thirteen years of age into the Church of England.

Both Sally and John had witnessed my baptism in 1981, in the Baptist Church in New Milton, which God had called me to, despite my Anglican status. John's baptism would have been fine, but, although Sally believed that God was calling her to be baptised with John, because she was an Anglican this could not be allowed, for the following reasons.

When the Anglican and Baptist Churches combined, a local Ecumenical project (the L.E.P.) was set up under the south Yorkshire sponsoring group. This group represented the two denominations, and had final authority on what was allowed. The rules about baptism were quite specific. It you had been baptised as an infant, but not confirmed, and wanted adult baptism as a believer, this was alright. After baptism you then became a Baptist in the L.E.P., Confirmation was seen as a public acknowledgement of the validity of baptismal vows which had been taken by others on behalf of the child, and was therefore a point of no return. Once confirmed, you could not be baptised within the L.E.P.

I can understand the difficulties they had. They were out in new territory, and they could not make exceptions. My baptism, with my vicar's permission, would hardly cause disruption in the Anglican Church, despite my previous confirmation. There were no rules as far as John Hayter knew, so I was able to obey God's calling, and still remain a member of the Anglican Church.

As I prayed for John and Sally, God made it clear to me that John would not find employment until he had been baptised. I told Sally and John, and, in desperation, Sally baptised John (as a temporary measure) in the bath! They both knew that this wasn't enough, but were not prepared for John to go ahead, and be publicly baptised on his own.

The services that they attended at Saint Thomas' were also fairly traditional. Sally knew that the church I worshipped with had a great deal more freedom and use of the spiritual gifts. There was spontaneous singing, dancing, tongues and prophecies, with clapping and hand raising. None of this seemed to exist at Saint Thomas'. They both began to feel restless. Surely there had to be more to belonging to the Church than they were experiencing? They discovered that a Community Church existed in Sheffield, so went along to their meetings.

It was a long way from their home in Crookes by bus on a Sunday, and often an even longer walk home. But they liked the people, and the worship. They discovered that they could be baptised together. So they left Saint Thomas' and joined the Community Church.

On Sunday, April 14th 1985, I witnessed their joint baptism in a swimming bath – it was a very happy event, and I enjoyed meeting their new Christian friends and worshipping and praying with them. Only a short time after his baptism, John found employment. God's word to me was fulfilled.

The Community Church served and cared for Sally and John in every way they could. When Sally had to go into hospital to have some lumps removed from a breast (they were non-malignant) the church ensured that she had transport there and back, and prayed and sat with her. They did the same when she had to have the cataract removed from her eye – a result of the cobalt radiation she had received as a child; how wonderfully this operation improved her sight. I was working full time, and lived a long way away, so I was very grateful that they received so much support.

However, Sally and John again began to feel restless. They were frustrated at having no function in the church. They wanted to serve as well as to be served. They knew that they had gifts which were not being used. They weren't too happy with the teaching on submission, and, were feeling pressurised about their lack of a family. Because of the genetic problems, and Sally's sterilisation, they could not have their own children. Adopting would be difficult as they were both partially sighted. They believed God had called them to be childless.

Back at Saint Thomas', a new development had taken place. A youth congregation was started, meeting at nine o'clock on Sunday evenings. Perhaps God was calling them back to Saint Thomas'? It would be another painful upheaval, but in December 1987 they decided to try this new service. They found the meeting exiciting, and sensed the power of God's presence. They realised that they could identify with this group, who were all their age, and who lived nearby in Crookes. Perhaps God would use their gifts more fully back at Saint Thomas'?

They got in touch with the church leaders, and one of them, Steve, came to talk to them, arriving on his motor bike, and sitting informally on the floor! Sally told me that the NOS (Nine-o-clock service) sometimes went on till after midnight, as the needs of the young congregation were met by fellowship and prayer.

I wanted to go to one of these services to find out exactly what was going on, but, as August was usually the month I visited Sheffield, I was unlucky; the congregation were always on holiday then. I did, however, meet some of the friends Sally and John had made in the church; they were young, idealistic, and very dedicated. They believed in living simply, so that far more than 10% of their salary (the usual tithe) could be given to God. Many had made great sacrifices to give all they could to the rebuilding of Saint Thomas'.

Their philosophy was simple – if you had more than one of anything you should give it away, otherwise you were robbing the poor. Perhaps someone needed your possessions more than you did – they should have them! It was a shock to find Sally and John with little furniture on one visit. We had to manage with cushions on the floor as they had given away their armchairs and sofa!

The N.O.S. group consisted of a very varied cross-section of the community, from highly educated graduates, to the young homeless and unemployed of the inner city.

To identify with these young people, the whole group abandoned any use of colour in their clothing, only wearing black, white or grey. It reminded me of the simplicity of the Quakers, as male and female alike, wore heavy black lace up shoes, black coats and jackets, black or white T shirts, etc. I was glad to get rid of everything black in my wardrobe for Sally to use, or to give to her young friends. Thankfully, the all black phase seems to be over now, and they are into colours again.

I could cope with the black clothing, but when I arrived on a weekend visit, and Sally greeted me, with her beautiful thick brown hair dyed black, and standing up in spikes all over her head, I could only gasp in horror and say,

'Sally, what have you done to your hair?' (I had always vowed that I would never criticise my children's taste in clothing, etc., as I had experienced this with my own mother – Oh dear!) Sally didn't seem to mind my comments – I managed to regain my composure and give her a hug – I would have to get used to the hair, the make-up too, thick black eyeliner, white cheeks, bright red lipstick! This identification with the inner city kids seemed to be going a bit far!

I had discovered that Sheffield was a beautiful city, set on seven hills. Buses were frequent and cheap. The city centre was laid out with large open walkways, trees and flowers. There were lovely parks, and, very near to Crookes – the open beauty of the Peak district. How I enjoyed visiting Hathersage – the family home of Clare Capron, the saintly woman in Brockenhurst, who had encouraged me with her prayers and poetry, when I first became 'born again'.

At last I visited Sheffield when the N.O.S. congregation

were meeting – I would be able to see for myself what happened. I wore navy trousers and a dark top, so that I wouldn't look too out of place.

Sally and John both liked to sit on the floor in the front, where there was a large empty space. I opted to sit on a seat just behind them, where I could have a good view. I made sure that I wasn't in front of a speaker, as, apparently the music was very loud!

The lighting was dim. People were rushing about, quietly sorting out the P.A. system for a large group of musicians who were assembling on the right. Huge photographs were projected onto the walls of the church all the way round.

The young people greeted each other with obvious affection. There was an air of expectancy and excitement. The church filled up, not only on the floor in the front, but all the chairs, the aisles and the balcony.

It was time to start. A young man walked to the microphone in the front – he needed a spotlight on him in the semi-dark church. Perhaps he was going to check the sound system? He had blue jeans on which were more holes than cloth, and on top, a cheap white, short-sleeved T shirt. No! he was speaking into the microphone – this was the start of the service!

After a few introductory words, the worship started. John and Sally had warned me that the music was loud, but I had never experienced anything quite like this. As the musicians started to play, a kind of roar seemed to go up from the congregation. The music started to reverberate through my chest, it was almost unbearable. How could I escape? I was held in by a crowd of young people on every side, all jumping up and down in time to the music. I decided that I would just have to join in. As soon as I started to move with the music, the discomfort disappeared! No wonder everyone was dancing!

I tried to concentrate on the words projected onto the wall in the front, hoping to become more involved. I realised that I wasn't enjoying this style of worship as much as the young people round me. It was extraordinary. I began to wonder what God felt about it?

As the service continued, I cried out,

'Please Father, is this type of worship what You want? Are You enjoying all this sound, and all these lighting effects?' I waited for an answer, then I became aware of waves of golden light pouring through the church, over the young people, and over me. I suddenly became lifted up into a glory that I had never before experienced. The glory of God's power, might, and majesty was present in the worship of these young people.

Where does it talk in the Bible about using loud cymbals, and trumpets? Of shouting for joy, and letting the sea resound? This was rather like being caught up in a resounding sea of glory.

God was showing me that, yes, He did enjoy this worship, it was right. He was a God of mighty sounds – thunder, the roar of the wind and the sea. He was a God of extraordinary lighting effects, rainbows, sunshine and clouds, lightning, and brilliant sunsets. He was enjoying the abandonment of noise and light and movement, in the worship of these young people.

I was very relieved – if God enjoyed it, who was I to complain? Later there were quieter moments, when we could sense the gentle presence of the Holy Spirit.

The young man in tattered jeans, gave a heartfelt sermon on the teachings of Jesus. There was a final message that anyone who needed prayer should stay in their seats. For everyone else, coffee, tea and soft drinks, were available in the lounge at the back.

Most of the congregation left the main worship area. The lighting in the lounge was also very dim. I wondered how Sally and John could ever see anything, with their limited sight!

After drinking tea, and chatting to some of the folks around me, I went back into the worship area to find Sally and John. There I saw people in small groups, deep in prayer, scattered over the area. God was indeed meeting their needs.

How careful we need to be, not to criticise and condemn the worship of others. We are all different, and God enjoys the variety of worship that we bring. As John Taylor the Bishop of Winchester wrote in his letter to me, 'The loving Creator never makes stereotypes.'

Worship comes from the heart, and can be contained in total silence, the gentle sounds of the countryside, the good old hymns and songs of the past, modern rock, jazz and blues, the mighty roar of an organ, dancing, etc . . . It is inadvisable for us to judge and condemn, as Michal did, when she saw King David leaping about, practically naked in full view of his people, as he rejoiced at the return of the ark. Michal was struck barren!

Is the ark of God returning to the Church in this country, welcomed by the uninhibited joy and delight of these young people? If so, they are the ones who will receive God's blessing in their lives, while those who condemn them, may, like Michal, find a barrenness and emptiness in their hearts and lives.

'David, wearing a linen ephod, danced before the Lord with all his might . . . .

Michal . . . . watched from a window. And when she saw King David leaping and dancing before the Lord, she despised him in her heart . . . .

When David returned home, ... Michal . . . . came out to meet him, and said, "How the King of Israel has distinguished himself today, disrobing in the sight of the slave girls . . . . as any vulgar fellow would."

David said ". . . . I will celebrate before the Lord.

I will become even more undignified than this . . . ."

And Michal, daughter of Saul had no children to the day of her death.'

(2 Samuel 6: 14, 16, 20, 22, 23)

137

'*Jesus replied, "Love the Lord your God with all your heart, and with all your soul and with all your mind."*'

(Matthew 22: 37)

3. The Future

What can I say to heal the hurt and pain of our divisions? I cannot produce theological arguments to prove that they are wrong. I know little of the entrenched doctrines that maintain our divisions. All I know is the suffering heart of God – His grief and pain that we do not love and accept each other, His sadness, that we are not one united body in Jesus.

I know too that in our weak and divided state, we are not the mighty force for good that we should be. We have access to all of Jesus' power and authority to turn back the tide of evil in our land and across the whole world. But the broken and divided body of the Church cannot wield this power in its weak and helpless state.

What can we do? How can we become one? There have been times when the Church has been united. In his book 'Priest in prison' John Hayter describes the meeting, for all the churches, that Bishop Wilson called in June 1942, in Singapore. Because of the war, people were dying in their hundreds, from dysentery, enteritis, and beri-beri. As a young anglican curate, John's task was to pack the dead bodies into a large communal grave. The poverty of the people of Singapore was terrible.

Bishop Wilson realised that the churches needed to work together to deal with the crisis, so a Federation of the churches of Singapore was established to relieve the poverty and distress of the people. The churches would keep to their own patterns of worship, but would be united in their Christian faith. They would have an agreed order of ministry, and would work together to relieve the suffering of the people. Here, in Singapore during the Second World War, was a time when Jesus' last prayer was answered – '*that they may be one.*'

Why did it happen here? It was because the need was obvious – the enemy was real. It was a war-torn land, and the people were in desperate need. Only a united Church could cope with organising the relief and help that could save the people from death.

As I write this in September 1990, another example of opposing institutions coming together to solve a crisis is taking place. President Bush of the U.S.A. and President Gorbachev of the U.S.S.R. are meeting together, burying their differences and past suspicions, to work together to free Kuwait from occupation by an invading agressor, Iraq. It is being said that a new era of world peace is being born through this unity of the two superpowers.

Because of the sacrifice of thousands of people in two world wars, we live today in freedom and peace in our land. There is plenty of food, there is good medical care and hygiene, law and order are established. We think that our need is not desperate. But isn't there a similar need, requiring unity in the Church, and the burying of past differences and suspicions?

If we look at the news on T.V. or read the daily papers, if we just listen to our friends and neighbours – we will hear of the pain of broken families, of divorce and separation, of illness and abuse, of unloved children, of the homeless, the unemployed, the lonely and the dying. We will read of violence and greed, cruelty, murder, suicide, theft and deception. We will be aware of drugs and alcohol abuse and of occult activities damaging minds and bodies.

Are we not also in a war-torn land? Aren't many of the people here just as desperate for help as they were in Singapore? Can we not see the effects of an invading aggressor? The people of Kuwait may never see Saddam Hussein, but they are suffering from the effects of his decisions – destruction, fear, hunger, and death. We may never see Satan and his demon host, but we can see the effects of their activities. The pain of broken hearts, minds and spirits can be just as terrible as that of broken bodies.

Can the government alter the situation by bringing in new laws? Would improved education, medicine, social care, housing, and employment radically change things? No, because the enemy is Satan, who is at work through his channels of human pride, selfishness, greed, lust, envy and fear. It is Satan who sets up the false gods of materialism and self-indulgence in a country where Christian values and teaching are ignored or forgotten by the majority of the population.

We are in a spiritual battle for our land; a new Battle of Britain, and it is only the Church that has the weapons to fight in this war. It is only a body of united Christians, filled with self-denying love, and holiness of living, who, through fasting and prayer, can wield the weapons that will disarm the enemy, and set the people free from Satan's bondage.

We need to seek the guidance and help of the Holy Spirit to enable us to know how to heal our divisions. Unless we set our own house in order, we are helpless in our attempts to resist the tide of evil pouring over our land.

> *'Jesus . . . . said to them ". . . . every city or household divided against itself will not stand."'*
>
> (Matthew 12: 25)

Our lack of fellowship and unity with other Christians, whatever their denomination, is unrighteous. We need to confess our sin, and repent of our unloving and judgmental attitudes.

> *'If we confess our sins, he is faithful and just, and will forgive us our sins and purify us from all unrighteousness.'*
>
> (1 John 1: 9)

To repent means to turn away from our sin. To go to those we have wronged and make amends for our lack of love and fellowship, for our pride and condemnation.

140

In his book 'In the Crucible',[1] Robert Warren suggests that the way forward in Church unity is by going back in repentance. He says that Anglicans need to repent of their treatment of Wesley and their persecution of Baptists. The Roman Catholic Church needs to repent of its treatment of Luther and the Reformers. He also says that 'rather than facing each other in conflict, the Church needs to be side by side on its knees, seeking to discover God's will, however costly that may be.'

Daily we pray '*Your Kingdom come, Your will be done on earth as it is in Heaven.*'

In heaven there are no divisions, no disunity. When we die and go to eternity with Jesus, all other Christians will be there, and we will be one with each other. Our theology, doctrine, traditions and personal opinions will be useless and forgotten. Our existence will focus on our oneness with Jesus, and we will be one with each other.

How can we say the Lord's prayer, then go out to perpetuate our separation from our Christian brothers and sisters? How can we refuse to fellowship and work with them? What hypocrites we are, to pray that God's Kingdom will come on earth, and God's will be done – then do our best to prevent it, by sticking to our entrenched traditions of doctrine and theology! May we start to pray, 'Your Kingdom come in me, Your will be done in me.'

It is so easy to blame other people for the lack of God's Kingdom on earth, but are we prepared to start bringing in God's Kingdom, by being changed ourselves? Are we willing for the Holy Spirit to convict us of our wrong attitudes, and our lack of love and humility? Will we allow Him to show us how little of the Kingdom of Heaven actually exists in our own hearts, and how much of our self-will we have still not submitted to the rulership of God?

'Forgive me Lord, and convict me of my sin towards Your Church.

[1] In the Crucible, copyright © Robert Warren 1989, published by Highland Books, Guildford.

Search me, and show me my fault.

Change me by breaking my pride and self-will.

Fill me with Your love for all my Christian brothers and sisters.

Give me Your humility in my dealings with them, and Your wisdom and understanding. Amen.'

Can we sincerely pray that prayer, with no reservations? If not, remember that Satan is the father of lies. He will do everything he can to work on our human fears, our weaknesses and our pride, to ensure that our divisions remain. The real enemy does not lie in dogma, doctrine, traditions and theology. We are being manipulated by Satan's host of demons, who seek to perpetuate our divisions.

> '*For our struggle is not against flesh and blood, but against . . . . spiritual forces of evil in the heavenly realms.*'
>
> (Ephesians 6: 12)

Are you now thinking, 'No, the demonic does not exist in me, or in my home, my church, or my town?' That is Satan's favourite weapon, to keep us in ignorance of his activities, and of his existence.

Is your Christian walk exactly as you would wish it to be? Are your family free from illness, worry, disharmony? Is your church flourishing?

If not, ask the Holy Spirit to reveal the underlying spiritual causes, and when you have found them, prepare yourself with other Christians for battle, dealing aggressively with the enemy by using the power in the name of Jesus.

> '. . . . *at the name of Jesus every knee should bow, in heaven and on earth and under the earth.*'
>
> (Philippians 2: 10)

Summary of ways to unite the Church

1. Repentance and forgiveness for past and present intolerance and separation in the Church.

2. Prayer and spiritual warfare, using the mighty name of Jesus, to free the Church of satanic oppression, and to release a new love and unity into the Church. (See Chapter 18).

3. Practical action, to enable us to pray, worship, and work together with other denominations. This already happens on a small scale, with combined prayer meetings, united services, Bible weeks and camps, national marches for Jesus, and evangelistic outreaches, when Christians like Billy Graham visit our country.

4. The difficult process of actually joining together separate denominations, as in Sheffield. This can happen when God gives churches a reason and a vision for unity.

Yes, the future unity of the Church lies in our growing desire to change and to repent, to forgive, and to have our eyes opened to the reality of the spiritual battle we are fighting. May we also support and pray for united church activities in our area, and, most of all, may we listen to the Holy Spirit, seeking God's will for the Church, and being obedient to the Spirit's prompting.

'Be completely humble and gentle; be patient, bearing with one another in love. Make every effort to keep the unity of the Spirit through the bond of peace. There is one body and one Spirit – just as you were called to one hope when you were called – one Lord, one faith, one baptism; one God and Father of all, who is over all and through all and in all.'

(Ephesians 4: 2–6)

'He who has an ear, let him hear what the Spirit says to the churches.'

(Revelation 2: 7)

18

The Need for Battle

The name of Jesus is powerful, as I have discovered from experience. Sometime in the late '70's, before I became a 'born again' Christian, I went to meet a 'guru' at a friend's house. She had invited him down from London. We all wanted to meet this man, so about a dozen of us arrived at her home. We sat in a circle on the floor of her darkened lounge.

The 'guru' was young, with a dark skin and long dark hair. He talked to us, explaining that he wanted us to bring God into the room. He said that this would be achieved by us all chanting 'Om'! I had no knowledge or experience of this kind of behaviour, and naively assumed that as there was only one God, the God of Abraham, Isaac and Jacob, it would be a good thing to do!

We sat and chanted, as the 'guru' walked round the circle behind us. He then stopped at one or another of us, and laying hands on us, spoke softly. When he did this to me, I sensed a strange excitement and shock going through my body.

I had forgotten about this experience, until I borrowed a book from the church library. It was called 'Death of a guru'. As I lay reading it in bed that night, I discovered that chanting 'Om' would not invoke God the Father, Jesus and the Holy Spirit, but a demonic god! I felt very disturbed, remembering my own involvement in this activity years before. I closed the book and took it downstairs – I didn't want it near me!

That night I had a terrifying nightmare. A demonic person was able to make me open a large box, from which menacing creatures emerged. The first time a frightening snake-like animal came out of the box, and it disappeared round a corner. The second time I saw another snake-like animal, and in my dream wanted to know what it was up to! So this time I looked round the corner. I saw it wrap itself round a man and kill him. It was horrible. The demonic person stood over me saying for the third time.

'Open the box.'

I knew that if I did, whatever came out of the box would now attack me. I was terrified – I started to say 'Jesus, Jesus, Jesus.' I woke up actually saying Jesus – the sound coming up from my throat.

I sat up in bed, sweating and fearful, and switched on a light. I knew the nightmare was related to what I had been reading, and was convinced that my experience of many years ago had in some way left an evil influence over me. How thankful I was that the name of Jesus had broken its power.

At 9 a.m. I rang May, who lived just down the road, and told her what had happened.

'Please would you pray with me. I need to be freed from this evil influence.' May was apprehensive.

'Can you wait till my husband comes home?' she said.

'No,' I replied, 'I am going out tonight – I only need your support, please let me come and see you now, I can't wait till tomorrow.'

By the time I got down to May's, she had found a book containing a prayer for self-deliverance. She gave it to me. I got down onto my knees, and started to read the prayer out loud. Something was trying to stop me! I struggled and fought to read the prayer through to the end. I made it. Then, whoosh, it was as if something lifted out of my head! I started to laugh – a great joy bubbling up inside me. Whatever it was had gone. I was free! Thank you Jesus! I was up on my feet, dancing up and down. May was relieved. It hadn't been as bad as she had feared!

Many years later I told Sarah about this experience (she

is one of my dear daughters in God). It wasn't long before she too found the truth of the power in Jesus' name.

During her first year as a drama teacher in a secondary school, she was asked to accompany a group of children to a Hindu temple in Southampton. They were to learn about the Hindu religion, as part of their education. Sarah could see no objection to this, though strangely the day of the visit coincided with her baptism, which would take place in the evening.

Sarah went to the temple with about sixty children and another teacher. The two R.E. staff were already there. At the door they all removed their shoes. The children enjoyed the novelty of this; padding into the temple in their socks, to sit in rows on the brown carpeted floor. There was a strong smell of incense in the air, and on the walls were large colourful pictures of the gods that Hindus worship. These included a picture of Jesus.

A beautiful woman in a long Indian dress entered, and said she would explain everything to them. She then gave the children time to ask the questions they had prepared. When they had finished Sarah asked,

'Why do you have a picture of Jesus on the wall, among all the other gods that you worship?' The woman replied,

'We believe that Jesus is a reincarnation of Krishna.'

Sarah began to feel confused. Was this woman right? Sarah was to be publicly baptised that evening, acknowledging that there is only one God, and that Jesus is His only Son. Yet this gentle and lovely woman was apparently convinced that Jesus was only one of many gods!

Another member of staff then asked for details of the ceremonies performed in the temple. The woman said that she would enact one for them.

In front of the children was an alcove covered with curtains. The woman pulled these back, revealing an altar in front of a statue of a Hindu god. One of the children was asked to hit two bells while the woman knelt down facing the altar. She raised her arms and started to pray to the god of that shrine.

Sarah began to feel very uncomfortable and frightened. Her breathing became difficult. She realised that she was reacting physically to something demonic. She had to do something quickly – but what? She then remembered what I had said about the name of Jesus.

As the woman knelt and prayed, Sarah started to quietly but urgently say, 'Jesus, Jesus, Jesus.' Within a few seconds the woman lowered her arms, stood up, and told the boy to stop hitting the bell.

'I'm sorry,' she said, 'but I can't go on, there must be some kind of spirit in this room, I felt my arms being pulled down.'

The other teachers asked,

'Is this because you are alone, without your husband present?'

'No.' she replied. 'I have often performed this ceremony, but today something in the room has stopped me. My arms were pulled down to my sides.'

Sarah said nothing. She knew that Jesus had answered her cry for help, and had stopped the ceremony. The fear and discomfort had left her, and the children in her care would not now be harmed. She also knew without any doubt that Jesus was more powerful than any Hindu gods, who were evil in nature.

That evening, Sarah wept as she publicly testified to the love and power of Jesus in her life and was baptised in the name of the one true God – Father, Son, and Holy Spirit.

Sarah had found for herself the power in the name of Jesus, and knew that it could prevent demonic forces from invading the innocent lives of the children in her care.

'Lord, forgive us for allowing our children to be exposed to so much that is harmful to their spirits – the violence, fear and crudity of many television programmes, pornography, the demonic in music and art and eastern religions, the occult activities of ouija

147

boards and tarot cards, role play games such as dungeons and dragons, all of which can lead them into bondage.

'Please Jesus, protect the children of our land from harm, not only to body and mind, but also to their spirits. Amen.'

Yes, there are demonic forces operating throughout our land. We need to ask the Holy Spirit to release us from our ignorance of Satan's activities, which disrupt and divide us, and damage and destroy mind, body, and spirit.

In a lead article in a local paper (February 22nd 1990) we read of children being drawn into the supernatural. A national report claims that three quarters of the country's school children dabble in the occult. The article describes some terrifying experiences of teenagers involved in levitation and ouija boards. It also states that there is a frightening growth in the numbers of teenagers indulging in fantasy role play. We hear on the news of twenty children being taken into care, to protect them from the ritual abuse of satanists.

Quite rightly there is an outcry if a dog bites a child at play, or if a child is abducted or abused. Everything is done to ensure that this will not be repeated. The dog is put down; the abductor is caught and punished. Yet the deep wounds to the minds and spirits of children drawn into occult activities go mostly unnoticed, save by a caring few.

How do you destroy an invisible enemy? How do you heal invisible wounds? Christian parents need to be on the alert. Most teachers today are not Christians, and they do not see any danger in Eastern religions, yoga, ouija boards, tarot cards, witchcraft, and fantasy role play. Find out what your children are being taught, and take action if you believe it is dangerous.

On the day that I write this – March 5th 1990 – parents of a boy in the church are concerned that their son is to go to a Hindu temple, to learn about the Hindu religion. They know that he will suffer in his work if he is withdrawn from this activity.

The group of 140 children have been told by an Anglican vicar, that it is perfectly alright for them to take part in the ceremonies of Eastern religions. He said, 'Hindus worship the same God that we do.'

'Jesus, what is happening in our land? Please turn back the tide of evil, threatening to engulf our children. Open the spiritual eyes of our Church leaders to the truth of Satan's activities.'

Are our homes the godly and secure havens they should be, allowing our children to grow in safety? Do Christian parents watch the children's programmes on T.V., and complain when the demonic is being portrayed?

It is in the home that children need to see Jesus uplifted, as they enjoy worship with singing and dancing. I discovered this when I visited Wally and Helen. It was a Sunday, and after tea Wally picked up his guitar, and we sang a worship song that his 8 year old son David had written.

Well, perhaps sang is the wrong description, as we ran around with the children, clapping and leaping, and jumping up and down like Jack in the boxes. I was out of breath at the end, but would recommend this for any Christian family who want to keep fit and healthy! After more energetic songs, Wally suggested a time of quiet worship from our hearts only and not our bodies. I was thankful to recover my breath as we sat and sang a gentle worship song, enjoying together the lovely presence of Jesus and the Holy Spirit.

It is no good expecting Sunday school and Church to teach children all they should know about Jesus. They need to be taught at home by reading Bible stories together, and by the family simply and naturally bringing their thankfulness and their problems to Jesus, in the secure knowledge that He will always care about the smallest detail of our lives.

We need to pray for the children of our land. As I was thinking of this, I was reminded of the people of Towyn in North Wales. Early in 1990 they had their homes damaged, and their possessions destroyed by the sea. Driven in by gale force winds and high tides, it entered through gaps in the sea walls to flood their homes. We saw and shared in their suffering, and admired their fortitude. To avoid further flooding the sea walls are being repaired. Lorry loads of huge boulders have been driven to the gaps. Men with diggers have lifted the boulders and filled the spaces in the walls.

Who will ensure that the protecting barriers round the shores of our children's lives are impenetrable? A tide of evil is entering the gaps to flood their hearts and minds. Will it be possible to clean up the resulting mess in the future, when the foundations of their minds and spirits have been damaged?

We cannot see or hear Satan at work; we only see the results of his activities in the suffering and pain in people's lives. Where are those who will stand in the gaps?

'I looked for a man among them who would build up the wall, and stand before me in the gap on behalf of the land so that I would not have to destroy it . . . .'

(Ezekiel 22: 30)

The gaps in our walls are there, and Satan can drive his destructive forces into our land. Where are the lorry loads of boulders, which are our united prayers? Where are the diggers and their drivers – those men and women who can discern where the gaps are, and move the boulders of prayer effectively?

Will we humble ourselves with fasting and prayer? Are we prepared to bear the repercussions which may result from standing up for what we know is right?

Are we watchful for our own purity of heart and mind, to move in the world, but not to take part in its ways?

Are we prepared to identify ourselves with the sins of other people, to take their shame to the cross, where their sins can be washed away as they are drenched in Jesus' blood?

In September 1990, Derek Prince came to preach at the Guildhall in Southampton. On the last night, Thursday September 6th, the church leaders on the platform led us in prayer. As an older man, Mr Owen, prayed for our land, the Lord said to me, 'You are to identify yourself with the sins of the people.' I then saw a picture of myself carrying a heavy sack on my back, I was bent double, then I walked outside the safe confines of life (the city gates) to a place of loneliness and pain, to the foot of the cross, and there I left my burden, for Jesus' blood to wash clean.

In Daniel chapter 9, we read how Daniel identified himself with the sin of the people.

(Verse 3). *'So I turned to the Lord God and pleaded with him in prayer and petition, in fasting, and in sackcloth and ashes.*

(4). I prayed to the Lord my God and confessed . . . .

(5). "we have sinned and done wrong. We have been wicked and have rebelled; we have turned away from your commands and laws."'

Yet we know from chapter 6 that three times a day, Daniel knelt and prayed, giving thanks to God (v.10) In chapter 10 verse 19 God called him a man who was highly esteemed. None of the sins that he confessed were his. He carried the sins of his people in his own heart, as Jesus did for us on the cross.

> *'And so Jesus also suffered outside the city gate to make the people holy through his own blood. Let us then go to him outside the camp, bearing the disgrace he bore.'*
>
> (Hebrews 13: 12–13)

Yes, I began to understand. Where the Church has fallen short in its self righteousness, and lack of love, I must take the blame, by humbly asking forgiveness.

How easy it is to be judgmental and unloving to those plagued by sin.

I realised that I must also identify with other sinners, as if their sin was mine, bringing their sin to the cross to receive Jesus' forgiveness and cleansing. I was to love and serve these people, hating only their sin and its originator Satan and all his demons.

Satan would dearly love us to leave his victims in the black and stinking pits that he has lured them into. In our fastidiousness, we would rather keep away from the disgusting stench of those who have been smeared with his hands. But underneath the mess is a man or woman suffering and longing to be clean and free, longing to know love, joy, and peace; to know hope instead of despair, to be free of misery, fear, hatred and discord.

> *'But God demonstrates his own love for us in this: While we were still sinners, Christ died for us.'*
>
> (Romans 5: 8)

> *'So from now on we regard no-one from a worldly point of view.'*
>
> (2 Corinthians 5: 16)

> *'And has committed to us the message of reconciliation.'*
>
> (2 Corinthians 5: 19)

> *'And who is equal to such a task?'*
>
> (2 Corinthians 2: 16)

> *'But thanks be to God, who always leads us in triumphal procession in Christ. . . .'*
>
> (2 Corinthians 2: 14)

Each person is loved by Jesus, and Jesus longs for us to be His ambassadors, reconciling the unclean to God, that they may be washed clean by the blood of Jesus.

Yes, there is a battle in progress for our land and its

people. The enemy's forces are drawn up on our borders. Satan is doing everything hc can to distract our attention, and to blind us to the truth of his activities. But if we are living in purity, close to Jesus, and listening to His word to us through the Bible, and directly through the Holy Spirit, then we have all the necessary equipment to rout the enemy. Let us prepare for spiritual battle, putting on the armour of light, and making our stand.

> *'Finally, be strong in the Lord and in his mighty power. Put on the full armour of God so that you can take your stand against the devil's schemes. For our struggle is not against flesh and blood, but against the rulers, against the authorities, against the powers of this dark world and against the spiritual forces of evil in the heavenly realms.'*
>
> (Ephesians 6: 10–12)

19

The Battle

1. Preparation – how to work together

How do we set about these spiritual battles? What should we do? Prayer meetings are often just lists of requests and thanks, under the guidance of a human leader.

Spiritual warfare is not like this. It takes place through small or large groups of people who '. . . . lean not on (their) . . . . own understanding' (Proverbs 3: 5), but who acknowledge the Holy Spirit as their leader, and are prepared to wait for Him to guide and instruct them, directly or through the Bible.

Christians who make a list of prayer needs, and plod through them as fast as possible to be sure nothing is left out, will never know the joy and excitement of spiritual warfare.

Group prayer warfare is effective when we love and trust each other, and trust that the Holy Spirit will lead us, and will speak to every person present. We need to be obedient to the Spirit's prompting, and however foolish we may feel, to speak out the thoughts that He puts into our heads. We then need to be humble enough to listen to, and acknowledge each other's anointing.

'. . . . *God chose the foolish things of the world to shame the wise; God chose the weak things of the world to shame the strong . . . so that no-one may boast before him.*'

(1 Corinthians 1: 27, 29)

In our prayer groups in Totton we are discovering that

spiritual warfare is sometimes like putting together a jig-saw puzzle. We are first given the pieces, then need to fit them together to see the picture, finally taking authority in the name of Jesus over evil forces revealed.

It is important for us to take authority, not to say 'Please Jesus, destroy or remove this evil'. Jesus has given us authority to do this.

'. . . . **Jesus** *gave them power and authority to drive out all demons* . . .' (Luke 9: 1), so we say 'I command you (naming the evil spirit) to go in the name of Jesus.'

When we started prayer warfare, we would find we were unable to deal with the demonic forces that we believed were present. Then we would realise that we hadn't put on our armour – God was protecting his forgetful children, and not allowing us into battle until we were prepared and ready.

> *'Therefore put on the full armour of God, so that when the day of evil comes, you may be able to stand your ground, and after you have done everything, to stand. Stand firm then, with the belt of truth buckled around your waist, with the breastplate of righteousness in place, and with your feet fitted with the readiness that comes from the gospel of peace. In addition to all this, take up the shield of faith, with which you can extinguish all the flaming arrows of the evil one. Take the helmet of salvation and the sword of the Spirit, which is the word of God. And pray in the Spirit on all occasions with all kinds of prayers and requests.'*
>
> (Ephesians 6: 13–18)

Every prayer warrior should learn this by heart.

When I first became a Christian I drew a picture of myself wearing the armour. It was a good way of ensuring that I remembered all the pieces. Though after reading 'Spiritual Warfare' by Derek Prince I realise that I made the shield too small. Derek believes that, like a Roman shield, it should cover the whole body.

And how about our unprotected backs? We all need our close Christian friends to protect us. It's surprising how you can see what the enemy is doing in someone else's life, but can be completely unaware of his strategy in your own!

We must not neglect to build up loving and close relationships with each other. Without these an energetic warrior could be cut off from behind, allowing Satan to undermine his or her credibility within the Church.

The Holy Spirit will alert us to the task of cleaning up people, buildings, cities and nations. I will include a few typical examples of the many battles we have waged in these areas.

2. Releasing People

The Lord alerts us to each other's needs. Sometimes we know in advance that a Christian brother or sister needs prayer, so we arrange to meet together specifically for that purpose.

This week, after fasting, I met with four women to pray for a situation that the Lord had shown us. We were to deal with an evil force, that for some time had damaged relationships in the church. It had also prevented the godly couple concerned from enjoying the love, peace, and joy that was their rightful inheritance.

As we prayed together, we each received different 'clues'. I saw a dragon with teeth bared. Another saw vicious and angry words coming from its mouth. A third saw the back of the throat with the uvula moving rapidly.

We knew that we were being asked to wield the sword of the Spirit to destroy this evil creature. I confess that we felt totally inadequate for this task, being reminded of Saint George and the dragon! Couldn't we just ask Jesus to destroy it? We put on our armour, and took authority in Jesus' name. Amazingly, we met no resistance, and had the joy of seeing this creature decapitated.

The Holy Spirit then alerted us to the need for healing of the past, and we prayed through the situations that had allowed this evil in.

The couple concerned will not need to know of our battle unless it seems right to share it with them. We haven't yet seen the outcome of our warfare, but, in faith, we believe a new joy will come into the church through this deliverance.

Other battles can bring more dramatic results. A year ago we met to pray for a Christian woman who had been behaving abnormally, and had been taken into a psychiatric hospital for treatment. She had come from abroad to study in our land, so was far from her own family and church.

As we prayed, the clues started to come. They were very odd; a chicken, the neck and back, witchcraft, a dark and demonic figure. One person in the group, who had lived in this country, then explained that chickens were sacrificed in certain witchcraft ceremonies. We then realised that the Holy Spirit was showing us that in this woman's childhood some rites had been performed that had left her under the influence of an evil spirit. We dealt in Jesus name with what had been revealed. Unfortunately one member of the group did not share a picture that she was given. She thought she was imagining it! We met to pray three days later in order to finish the battle.

Only a day or two after this, the woman was released from hospital, completely well! Other people in the ward were so amazed by her rapid cure, that they started to come to her for advice and prayer.

This type of prayer is only part of the ongoing release that all Christians experience as we are '. . . . being *transformed into his likeness with ever increasing glory . . . .*' (2 Corinthians 3: 18).

New Christians with deep traumas from the past may need many months of prayer and deliverance, as one layer after another of Satan's deceptions are removed, bringing wholeness to mind, body and spirit.

157

A woman who joined our Church shortly after her conversion, has needed two years of prayer and deliverance. She suffered from Menieres disease, which affected her hearing and balance. She had been unable to lead a normal life when coming under its attacks, and there was no known medical cure. We were shown that the roots of this disease lay in the sexual abuse she suffered as a child. She received prayer and counselling from many different people, and groups, and from well known church leaders.

Some people were sceptical, suggesting that she was imagining her symptoms! She, however, knew her own needs, and I was given the grace not to get impatient, or to doubt her requests for more prayer. We did reach a point when she was always looking to me to solve her problems, and I knew I must withdraw, so that she would turn directly to Jesus.

Slowly she has changed from a fearful and sick woman to a radiant and healthy Christian, who is now able to minister to others. Seeing the changes in her, both her husband and daughter have now become Christians.

We all long for more souls to come into the Church, but recently, as we prayed for an evangelistic outreach that we were planning, the Lord spoke to me. This was part of what He said:

'Put aside the pretence and open your hearts to each other, confessing your sins and your needs.

Humble yourselves and serve each other with all that you have, that I may walk in your midst, and shed My love abroad to draw in a mighty harvest.

If it is lost souls that you seek, do not cry out for these, but first cry out for yourselves, to be on fire with My love, My compassion, My tenderness, and My holiness. Then I can bring the increase, I can bring the harvest.

For I would not have My new born babies confused and rejected, crying for warmth, for comfort, for food, for love.

Even the birds first prepare the nest, and warm the eggs and diligently sacrifice themselves to feed the young. Yet your nest is bare and cold, and many cry and toil alone.

Love one another as I have loved you, and pray for one another that I may bring in the harvest.'

At a recent prayer meeting, after I had read this aloud, we knew that we should pray for each other rather than for world issues, etc. It was extraordinary to discover the deep needs in each person present. One person was delivered from lying spirits, that had been placing despondency and disillusionment about Christianity in her heart and mind. The next day she was able to visit an unsaved neighbour, and offer to pray for her. She has since been filled with a new joy and faith.

Yes, if we pray for one another, openly sharing our needs, our anxieties and fears, our joys and sorrows, then our love and commitment to each other will grow. Outsiders will be able to say of us, as they did of the early disciples 'See how these Christians love one another.'

In John 13: 35, Jesus said, '*All men will know that you are my disciples if you love one another.*'

Our joy and love will overflow to our neighbours and friends. There will be no need for big evangelistic rallies; people will be drawn into the warmth and life that we radiate. The Holy Spirit will 'bring in the harvest.'

'*May the Lord make your love increase and overflow for each other and for everyone else. . . .*'

(1 Thessalonians 3: 12)

'. . . . *serve one another in love. The entire law is summed up in a single command: "Love your neighbour as yourself."*'

159

'Carry each other's burdens, and in this way you will fulfil the law of Christ.'

(Galatians 5: 13, 6: 2)

3. Releasing buildings

In the summer of 1988, I went on holiday to Cornwall with Sarah and Karen. We rented a cottage in a valley on the North coast.

It was a beautiful spot, wild and lonely, with a view of the sea. We took Sarah's dog Poppy, and walked for miles across the bare, boulder strewn hills surrounding the valley.

One day, during our first week, Karen and I took Poppy for a walk to enjoy the sunset, leaving Sarah alone in the cottage reading a book.

It was getting dark when we returned, and we were surprised to find that Sarah was feeling very frightened. While she had been sitting reading in the living room, she said that a black and evil presence had entered, and stood near her. She had only kept it at bay with the name of Jesus, and prayer. She was so relieved to have us back home again.

We had been unaware of anything wrong with the cottage, though we knew it was very old. To allay Sarah's fears I suggested that we should pray in each room, banishing anything evil.

Karen and Sarah were fairly new Christians, and had never experienced spiritual warfare. They looked scared at the idea. I explained to them that we had nothing to fear, because we had complete power and authority in the name of Jesus. We were His disciples, and He had given us His authority to use against any evil powers that we might encounter, though we first needed to go through a pre-battle routine of personal cleansing by the blood of Jesus, and then put on our spiritual armour. This would ensure that we were completely safe. We could then have victory over any powers of darkness, through the power

160

of Jesus. They rather nervously agreed, and we prepared ourselves for battle.

We started in the living room and moved to the kitchen, then to the bathroom, the hall, stairs, landing, Karen's room, my room. It all seemed quite peaceful. I was beginning to decide that Sarah's imagination had been working overtime.

The last room that we prayed in was Sarah's. It was the largest bedroom, with a lovely view down the valley to the sea. We stood round her bed praying, and suddenly I saw it, – a huge black and menacing figure standing in the corner. Sarah was right, there certainly was something evil in this house. I told them what I could see, and we took authority in the name of Jesus. After a short battle, whatever it was left the house.

Phew! We all breathed a sigh of relief, especially Sarah, who hadn't been sleeping very well. The house certainly felt very different afterwards. (We didn't tell anyone in Cornwall about our battle). Karen decided to return for another holiday at the end of the year to 'see in' 1989. She rented a cottage for three a little further down the same valley.

On New Year's Eve, Karen, Ruth and Sharon, walked down to the village pub. All the locals were gathered there, including the landlady, who owned the cottage in the valley.

The locals wanted to know where Karen and her friends were staying, so Karen explained that they were in a cottage up the valley.

'Oh, which one?' they asked.

When Karen gave the name, they were relieved.

'We're glad it's that one,' they said, 'the cottage farther up the valley is haunted!'

Karen discovered that they were talking about the cottage we had rented in the summer! The landlady spoke up,

'I never go into that house alone, I'm far too frightened, so my husband and the dogs have to come with me.' (She hadn't warned us of this in the summer!) She said that a friend of hers had stayed for a while in the cottage, and although he was not alone, he said he would never stay there again. He had found it very frightening.

The locals started to laugh and joke with each other, as they thought of the tourists, who paid to stay in a haunted house each summer!

Karen with great courage spoke out to the assembled locals.

'I stayed in that cottage for two weeks in the summer with two friends. We realised that the cottage was haunted, so we prayed in every room. You'll find that it isn't haunted any more. We're all Christians, you see.'

The New Year festivities suddenly halted, and there was a stunned silence throughout the pub!

She then asked the landlady if she had been in the house since we had left.

'Yes,' she said, 'but not on my own.'

'Well, you'll find that its alright to be alone there now,' said Karen. 'Whatever was haunting that house has definitely gone!'

Later this experience proved useful, when Karen went to look after her old and ailing dog for a few days. It meant she was sleeping alone in her mother's house.

As we drove back to my house one night, Karen started to say that she was finding it difficult to sleep because, despite full central heating, and lots of bed clothes, she was unable to keep warm in bed. She had remembered Sarah not sleeping well in Cornwall, and had always felt a darkness and oppression in her mother's house. Was it an evil influence?

We decided to turn round and go back to the house, despite the late hour. It was 11pm. We prepared for battle, then started to pray in each room. We quickly became aware of evil forces in many of the rooms, and took authority over them in Jesus' name. When we had finished going round the house, we still felt uneasy. Perhaps we should pray for the garden? There used to be an old well there which was the source of water for the original inhabitants.

As we prayed (I was amazed to hear Karen boldly taking authority. I hadn't realised that a relatively new Christian could learn so quickly), an evil presence left the well. We felt great relief and knew that our task was completed. Next day, Karen noticed a lot of disturbance round the site of the old well, as if a wild animal had been thrashing about.

When her mother returned, she told her what had happened. Her mother then told Karen that many years before, a woman had been cooking in a lean-to kitchen at the back of the house. She had accidentally set her clothes on fire, and in desperation, had jumped into the well (the only source of water) and had been drowned!

When Karen came downstairs, the morning after the battle, having had a warm and comfortable night's sleep, she found the whole house flooded in golden sunlight, and all the sensations of darkness and oppression had gone.

Children are often very sensitive to evil forces in a house. One evening a large group of Christians were praying together in a leader's house, and we became aware of the presence of a demonic force. We had many prayer burdens that night, so there wasn't time to deal with this before we left.

Later I discovered that the couple's 11 year old son had a history of disruptive behaviour, and had developed a bad reputation in his junior school. He had just moved to a new school, and the parents were concerned that his behaviour was getting worse due to the bad company he was keeping.

Some time later I visited them again for prayer. We had a lovely evening, finishing with mugs of tea and coffee. The mother then reminded me that I had suggested praying round the house when I next visited them. Oh dear, I had completely forgotten! Leaving the others, I quickly went through the house with her. It all seemed fine, until we got to the last room which belonged to her youngest

163

son! There was something really evil here. We started to pray, but it was a big one; we needed reinforcements!

I went back to call in the 'heavy mob' – the two church leaders and their wives. It was an exciting battle, and whatever it was, left the room. The boy had slept for 8 years in this room, and when he was small, often had nightmares. It would take time for him to be healed from such a long contact with an evil force, especially as it took place when he was asleep and at his most vulnerable.

Shortly after this he started to talk to his parents openly about his activities, and his disruptive behaviour at school began to diminish.

People's homes are not the only buildings that may need to be 'cleaned up'. A year ago, the Holy Spirit alerted me to evil forces over a local school.

It all started through my dog, Benji, a 7 month old golden cocker spaniel. He needed daily walks, and usually had a good run after breakfast. However one morning it was pouring with rain. I decided it would have to be a quick walk away from the mud and wet ditches, so we walked round the allotments opposite my house. This walk involved passing a middle school for 8 to 12 year olds. Some of the children were already making their way to school.

As I walked along the back of the school, I became aware of sickness in my stomach, tightness in my chest, and difficulty in breathing. I knew that I was responding physically to the presence of evil forces in or over the nearby building. I started to feel angry; here were children, innocently waving goodbye to their mothers and fathers, to go into a building that was in some way under Satan's control!

The next day was dry and sunny, but I decided to walk the same way. It was later, so more children were about, and I realised that I knew several of the children attending this school. Most of them were from Christian families. The matter was now becoming more urgent, but I had to be sure.

Again on the third morning, I walked past the school. The Holy Spirit wanted me to walk all round the school praying in tongues.

I hadn't realised that this was possible, but discovered a path round an adjoining football pitch, which took me onto the road in front of the school. I prayed along this route binding the evil forces, and claiming protection for both the staff and the children.

As I completed the circuit, I sensed opposition. It was quite an effort to continue to pray in tongues, and fill in the final gap. The prayer group said that they would come and pray over the school on the following Monday, and until this happened, I knew that I must continue to pray round the school each morning.

Meanwhile Gillian, the mother of two children attending this school, called in to see me. She told me of several disturbing things that had been happening at the school. These included a great deal of occult activity among the children, with the use of ouija boards, and attempted séances. There were also stories of ghosts in the school, and the children were frightened of visiting one of the outer buildings, where a 'ghost' was said to be present.

Even in the classroom evil influences were present in some of the teaching ideas and materials used. Gillian's daughter was put into an 'acid house group' until her mother objected. When the topic 'Power' was studied, the power of evil was included, with teaching on witchcraft. There was no mention of the power of God!

The prayer group met together on the Monday. After preparing for battle we walked to the school, and sang and prayed round it until we were sure that the battle had been won, and any evil forces over the school had been dispersed.

Shortly after this a new deputy headmaster was appointed who was a Christian. I was able to go to a Harvest Festival service there and felt a great joy and peace for the children, as the new deputy led the singing of some inspired Christian songs.

Now, about a year later, there is little evidence of any occult activity among the children.

Another school for older children nearby has needed prayer, after several frightening experiences among the children, during the use of ouija boards.

Parents, please ask the Holy Spirit to help you to pray effectively for your children's schools, and do not allow them to be involved with activities which will damage their spirits.

4. Releasing towns and cities.

If the Church is to flourish, we also need to battle in prayer against the principalities and powers over towns and cities, that resist the work of the Holy Spirit. This resistance may be long established, and rooted in pagan worship and rituals of long ago. Local covens of witches and other occult activities in the area may be reinforcing the demonic strongholds.

Until we have broken the power of Satan over an area, we cannot expect the gospel to be effective in leading people to Jesus, and the divisions and disunity in the Church to be healed.

Why is it that in our land such a small number of people believe in Jesus? It isn't because we don't have enough churches. Many of the small minority of Christians are actively working and evangelising. Then what prevents the Gospel being received?

I believe that the power of Satan is at work to blind the eyes, and stop up the ears of our neighbours, families, and friends. We need to fight together against the forces that brood over the towns and cities of our land.

Recently the Totton group have battled in prayer for a nearby town. This major warfare, which was against a 'ruler of darkness', required preparation through a deep commitment to prayer and fasting. For seven weeks we sought guidance from the Holy Spirit; we asked Him to reveal to us the demonic forces that we believed were at work.

It was at the beginning of January that I was first alerted to the existence of these dark forces. I was visiting friends for dinner, and, as we chatted, Jane confessed that she always felt afraid and oppressed by evil, when inside the parish Church. I knew that Jane was spiritually very sensitive. I also knew that the church in this town was facing difficulties, and seemed to be making little progress. Was there a connection between dark forces over the town, and the problems in the church? I started to investigate (for this part of the work, you need to be something of a detective!)

Sarah works in a school near the church. She told me that on one dark evening she had walked alone round the church, and was terrified by the awareness of an evil presence. I consulted Dave about this. He saw a picture of a 'brooding power of darkness', over the cross in front of the church.

Karen then told me of some strange occurrences that had taken place in this church fourteen years ago. One of her friends sang in the church choir, and had twice been frightened by inexplicable events taking place at choir practice. For example, the sound of a violent storm outside, yet when they left the building it was a perfectly clear and calm night. On another occasion, they heard a baby wailing in the church, but there was no-one else there.

Karen's friend Debbie told her of a young man, who had boasted of taking part in occult activities in a room very close to the church.

Armed with this information, we started to pray, and at a meeting on Monday January 29th were given three 'pictures'. The first came as Paul read from the word. He saw a sword with limitless power coming down towards Satan's neck. Marie saw a large and very old stone. A bright light shone down on it, and it flicked over, revealing a mass of black demonic creatures that rushed to get away. Dave then saw four huge angels, each about a mile high, standing on the four sides of the town, holding swords up in an arch, their points touching. They were waiting for the command to bring them down, to strike the evil creature.

When I realised the enormity of the battle ahead, I was astonished that God was asking our little insignificant band of humans in Totton to command such enormous angels! God then reminded me that it takes only a small key to start a car, and a small match to light a fire. Without the key, a car is useless, and without a match, the fire won't light.

We were liaising with the elders of our sister church in this town, and I was given two scriptures for them.

'But if you do not drive out the inhabitants of the land, those you allow to remain will become barbs in your eyes and thorns in your sides. They will give you trouble in the land where you will live.'

(Numbers 33: 55)

'The weapons we fight with are not the weapons of the world. On the contrary, they have divine power to demolish strongholds.'

(2 Corinthians 10: 4)

We arranged to visit the town on February 16th, to deal with this ruler of darkness, preparing ourselves by prayer and fasting.

Before this visit, on Sunday, February 11th, I visited Sarah. She had fallen from her horse. As I talked to her I felt disturbed, she looked so strange. I knew that something was badly wrong. I sensed that an evil power had been involved in her fall. But why?

Sarah was a prime target. In her work as a teacher, she frequently witnessed to the children of this town, praying for them, and encouraging the young Christians. She had an acute spiritual sensitivity, but for several weeks had not

168

attended Sunday worship or midweek meetings. Without the covering and fellowship of other Christians, Satan had been able to attack her.

When we met on Monday February 12th for prayer, I told the group about Sarah and her fall. We prayed, and Dave was shown that a 'tentacle' had reached out from the evil power over the town, and was holding on to her. Afterwards, Sarah said she was aware of not being properly in control of her horse, and felt as if she was pulled backwards when she fell off.

We cut her free from the 'tentacle' in the name of Jesus, and Rosalyn prayed the covering power of Jesus' blood over her. Dave then 'saw' the blood of Jesus going up the severed tentacle into the demonic being and enraging it! We knew that we couldn't wait until Friday to destroy the evil creature, but that it would have to be dealt with immediately!

Eight of us joined hands in a circle and prayed in tongues. Dave then saw the four swords held by the huge angels, slashing down to cut the evil power into four pieces, which then shrivelled and died. As the swords hit the ground, big sparks shot out in every direction – moving through the surrounding dark areas of the town. We sensed the victory, and full of joy, sang songs of praise to God.

On Friday, February 16th, we fasted, and nine of us met together to prepare ourselves for battle, by prayer, reading and declaring out the Word, breaking bread, and putting on the armour. We drove to the town, meeting up with three local Christians (others were fasting and praying at home). We walked round the church together, singing songs of victory and praise. We then walked to the cross in front of the church.

There was a biting cold wind, and we were glad that we had put on warm winter clothes. We sang and worshipped, then started to pray. Marie stopped our prayers, saying that we needed to continue to worship God to lift the powers of darkness. During the previous week, Janet and I had found the words 'Praise is an act of warfare', which we knew was the key to the evening. We did as Marie suggested.

Slowly the atmosphere round us changed, and the holiness of God came down over the area. Three of us knelt on the stone paving. Then we 'saw' the big stone being turned over, and the black demons below were shrivelled up in the heat as they tried to rush away.

Paul suggested that the three Christians from the town should be prayed over, as representatives of the church there, so they stood in the centre of the circle. While in Totton, Dave had a picture of an unlit candle by the cross. As we prayed, we knew that the three Christians were like three flints. Together they generated a spark which lit the candle. We knew then that God's light could now shine in this town in a new way, and that the demonic superpower had been destroyed.

In April we were asked to speak to a group of men and women from the church who wanted to learn more about intercession. All the elders were present. I had prepared a list of guidelines on prayer warfare, based on our experiences in Totton, and handed out copies.

Guidelines for Prayer Warfare

The Holy Spirit cannot be confined to a set of rules, and is constantly revealing new things. The following is an outline of some of the strategies that we at present are putting into practice.

Always be prepared for the Holy Spirit to do the unexpected.

See Jesus in victory in every situation, and do not be afraid of the enemy, he has been defeated by the blood of Jesus. Alleluia!

1. About six to ten Christians meet together, bringing prayer needs. A Church leader is present or covering the group.
2. The room should be comfortable, and not too brightly

lit, with space in the middle, and enough chairs, or cushions on the floor, so that you can be free to stand, kneel, walk about, lie down, etc, as the Holy Spirit directs.

3. Start with worship and thanksgiving, including songs, hymns, reading from the Word, prayers of praise, etc. (This is often interspersed in the warfare)

4. Declare your love and trust for each other, ensuring that any anxiety, fear or disharmony in the group is dealt with. If it is a new group, the Holy Spirit may need to spend time healing fears and hurts within the group, through repentance, forgiveness, and love, with the laying on of hands and prayer.

5. Put on the armour (Ephesians 6: 14–18) and claim the protection of Jesus' blood for your families, homes, and everyone present in the house.

6. Discard all human knowledge of known needs, allowing the Holy Spirit to prompt the prayers, as you give the whole time to Him. '. . . . *the Counsellor the Holy Spirit . . . will teach you all things. . . .*' (John 14: 25).

Ask Him to come among you saying, 'Holy Spirit, we invite you to come and lead and guide us.' Then wait for Him to speak to you.

7. The Holy Spirit will give you information; this is where your love, trust and humility operate. It is often only one word, or a picture or a physical sensation, which you won't understand. Be prepared to speak out exactly what you are receiving, trusting that someone else in the group can complete the picture. However foolish it seems, share it; if you hold back, much time may be wasted.

8. When the 'diagnosis' is complete, pray and supplicate; that is, one person may start to cry out and weep, as they plead before God. (Have tissues handy). Pray in tongues until the moment of victory, when one or two people take authority in Jesus'

171

name. This means telling the enemy to go in the name of Jesus, not asking Jesus to do it. He has given us the authority.

When dealing with a big issue it is effective for all to stand in a circle holding hands, praying in tongues.

9. A sense of joy and release indicates that the victory has been won. If this doesn't come, continue to pray.

10. After the victory, praise and worship God, giving Him the glory before the next battle. If it's a long session, have a drink and a rest before continuing.

11. If you are contesting a major force, e.g. 'a ruler of darkness' over a town or city, fast, then take bread and wine together, to be strengthened for the battle. You may need to spend time in fasting and prayer during the weeks before the battle.

12. Ask the Holy Spirit to show you how to proceed in a big battle. He will show you whether the battle can be fought in your home, or if you should go to the area where the evil force operates. Praise is an act of warfare, and may be the most important part of the battle as you walk or stand together, worshipping God, and lifting Jesus up in victory over the area.

The Lord also gave me Psalm 133:

(v.1). '*How good and pleasant it is when brothers live together in unity!* . . .

(v.3). . . . *For there the Lord bestows His blessing.*' God was saying to them, and to all of us, that it is only when we are working together in love, unity, and harmony, that we will be blessed, and the Church prosper.

After going through the guidelines, we prayed together, especially for a new love to grow between them all, and for the church to go forward together in that town.

It was good that the church leaders were present; they need to be involved in major warfare, providing their covering and authority, to protect the flock. Satan will do everything he can to bring misunderstanding and opposition to undermine the heartfelt efforts of the most godly prayer warriors. Intercessors need the support of their church leaders. Swimming out into the deeper waters of group prayer warfare and intercession is exciting but can be dangerous without proper preparation and covering.

Prayer warriors should not just meet together for intercession. There needs to be a knitting of hearts in our daily lives, through a sharing of burdens, through fellowship, fun and laughter. The Holy Spirit showed us that one church group alone cannot deal with all the satanic superpowers in an area. We were made aware that some powers over Totton would not be dealt with until the different denominations pray, worship, and work together.

On Good Friday of this year (1991) we all joined together for a march of witness through Totton. Three large crosses were carried from separate points in the town, followed by members of the different churches. We met to hammer them into a small grassy hill in the centre of the town, and then we prayed and sang together.

On the following Monday when our prayer group met as usual, we were given a new burden of intercession for Totton. Our march together was somehow enabling us to break through the powers of darkness over the town.

There are deeply entrenched spirits of religion over many of our towns and cities, making dogma more important than Jesus, and preventing the flow of love between Christians that would break down the denominational barriers. These barriers are an abomination to God. May we seek the guidance of the Holy Spirit, and prepare ourselves to bind these spirits, and release the Church from its divisions.

May we become intercessors, whatever the cost in terms of personal inconvenience, when necessary giving up our time, our sleep, and our food, to restore our land and its people to God, and to bring the healing love of Jesus to our Church, and to our nation.

Can we embrace the cross of sacrificial prayer? It

can only lead to the joy of resurrection, as we see people freed from Satan's bondage, and the Church becoming powerful and strong, a mighty force for good in our land.

Jesus said, *'If anyone would come after me, he must deny himself and take up his cross daily and follow me.'*

(Luke 9: 23)

Free the Church

We free it in Your name,
from all the pride and prejudice,
from all the fear and shame,
from centuries of Satan's chains,
that all, new life may gain.

Free the Church

From all those principalities
the powers of darkness deep,
that brood above our nation,
   and in our Churches
keep division and confusion,
Your sword to lie asleep.

Free the Church

We come against you Satan,
in Jesus' mighty name,
We wield the sword, His Word to us,
to put your ranks to shame,
dishonour to your evil plans,
God's Church on earth will reign.

Free the Church

Then beautiful His Bride will be,
In robes of spotless white,
Her jewels shining in the sun,
Her diadem so bright,
as all united we shall be,
in everlasting light.

The Church will be free.

20

Israel, the Jews and Church Unity

Why was I on an El Al flight to Israel for a four week study tour in November 1990? Most other groups had cancelled, yet I knew that it was important that we went, even though Saddam Hussein was threatening to attack Israel.

I later discovered that the Lydias were involved in intercession for the Jewish people and Israel. It was a great joy when the Holy Spirit gave us a burden to pray for Israel. God unexpectedly opened my eyes to this need, at the end of the tour.

Meanwhile, God assured me that we would come to no harm, and would return safely; that we would be a light in the darkness as we travelled round Israel, and that our prayers and presence there were important. He gave me the verse from Esther – 'You are going to Israel for such a time as this' (Esther 4: 14). He also said that I would learn something important for my book. What would it be? I didn't understand how walking in Jesus' footsteps would teach me anything about Church unity!

I knew nothing about Israel, and had taken little interest in the Jewish people during their long struggle for survival, though I knew that God still had a great love for them.

I learnt this on a trip to Switzerland. During our stay in Gstaad, we visited an exhibition of paintings by an artist called Dan Rubinstein. As we walked round we discovered that many of his paintings were illustrations of stories from the Old Testament. One in particular of

King David's lyre, with the Hebrew text of Psalm 150 flowing through the strings, captured my interest.

Who was this man? I consulted the brochure. He was a Jew, who came to Gstaad to paint and exhibit his work each year.

We went to the desk to buy cards of the paintings. Dan was sitting there, and we talked to him. He was short and thin, his body crippled by disease. His large brown eyes were searching and expressive. He could speak several languages including English. Looking at him it seemed to me that the suffering and pain of the Jewish nation filled his eyes, and was imprinted on his body. If only he knew Jesus as we did. We told him that we were Christians and that we loved the Jewish people; they were the chosen nation of God, through whom Jesus had come.

But as we spoke I was puzzled. I hadn't met a Jewish person before. Why did I feel such a love for this man? Why was I telling him that the Jewish nation were special to God? Several years later I was to find the answer in Israel.

Israel was exciting. For the first three weeks of our visit we went on a biblical tour, starting with three days in the desert, sleeping in a bedouin tent, riding camels, learning what it was to pant for the living water.

We spent two weeks in Jerusalem at the Christchurch hospice in the Old City. We became aware of the powerful forces at work in Jerusalem. It was as if a huge spiritual battle was being waged over the city between the power of Islam and Jesus.

Later we stayed by the Sea of Galilee. It was beautiful to be aware of Jesus and His gentle but powerful presence by the lakeside and in the countryside.

It was our final weekend in Jerusalem. At last we were to hear something about modern Israel. First an Arab Christian spoke to us of reconciliation between Arab and Jew through Jesus. Then a Messianic Jew, Reuben Berger, spoke to us.

As I listened I was astounded. I had always thought that the Church was the new Israel, and Jerusalem would be built 'in England's green and pleasant land'.

Reuben expounded the Biblical prophecies about Israel. He said that God was restoring Israel, which wasn't the Church, but the Jewish nation, and the actual city of Jerusalem was still important in God's plans!

I remembered that as we first drove into Jerusalem I had unexpectedly started to weep, and was surprised to realise that Jesus still weeps over Jerusalem.

What I had understood to be just a spiritual Jerusalem and Israel, was being outworked in the material in a real place, and at a real time – now!

Wow! Scales seemed to fall from my eyes. Then, what was he saying?

'Unity will not come to the Church until the initial break between God and Israel is healed . . .

Israel is a stumbling block to the Church. The restoring of a proper relationship between Jew and Gentile will bring about healing for the whole body of Christ . . .

Through Israel being grafted back onto the olive tree, God will bring ultimate blessing to the world and unification to the Church.'

This was it. God had said I would learn something important for Church unity in Israel. His word to me was being fulfilled. We were to pray for Israel, for the Jewish people, to be grafted back. Through this the Church would be united!

A week after I returned to England I collected the films I had taken in Israel. I excitedly opened the packet. As I spread out the photographs I suddenly realised that I had been witnessing the fulfilment of biblical prophecy. (During that week I had been re-reading the prophets, Isaiah, Jeremiah, Micah, Zephaniah, Joel, Zechariah, Ezekiel etc.) I had photographed these prophecies actually taking place!

There were the Jewish bride and groom, beautifully dressed in their bridal garments, walking and talking together as they were being photographed at the Western Wall. In Jeremiah it said,

178

'. . . . in . . . the streets of Jerusalem . . . will be heard once more . . . the voices of bride and bridegroom . . . .'
(Jeremiah 33: 10–11)

I gazed in wonder at the picture of the three little Jewish girls, looking so pretty in their best party dresses, with crowns of paper flowers on their heads. I had got Margret (my room-mate) to hold them for me to take a photograph. They excitedly talked to us in Hebrew, and a passer-by explained that they had just been to a party. These children, like their ancestors, had been born here. This was their home, they knew no other.

'Their children will be as in days of old. . . .'
(Jeremiah 30: 20)

Behind them was the clean, elegant, newly built Jewish quarter that had been totally demolished.

'. . . . I will resettle your towns, and the ruins will be rebuilt.'
(Ezekiel 36: 33)

'. . . . the city will be rebuilt on her ruins. . . .'
(Jeremiah 30: 18)

I looked at my photographs of the kibbutz we had stayed in. Jeremiah prophesied 2,500 years ago that:

'He who scattered Israel will gather (kabbetzin) them. . . .'
(Jeremiah 31: 10)

He had known that the people would live together in kibbutz when they returned to Israel from all over the world.

When the kibbutz started, the Jewish immigrants worked hard for little reward. My neighbour, Frank, was in Israel in 1946, and was astonished to see the

Jewish people planting row upon row of seedling trees –
banana, date, lemon, orange, grapefruit, pineapple etc.,
and laying out vineyards.

'But it will take years for you to get any harvests!' he
said.

Today their children reap the reward of their parents'
labour, and the prophecy of Amos is being fulfilled.

'. . . . *They will plant vineyards and drink their wine;
they will make gardens and eat their fruit.*'

(Amos 9: 14)

One of my photographs was of a kibbutz in the desert
of the southern Jordan valley. There were many of these
big green areas scattered along the dry, and yellow, sand
and rock filled valley. As Isaiah had said,

'*The desert and the parched land will be glad; the wilder-
ness will rejoice and blossom. Like the crocus, it will burst
into bloom; it will rejoice greatly and shout for joy.*'

(Isaiah 35: 1–2)

Yes, the green and fertile kibbutz were 'shouting for
joy' in the desert.

I had two photographs of shops in the Jewish quarter of
the Old City, so clean and well laid out. Margret and I had
decided to buy a simple lunch of bread and fruit, having
tired of the rich 'falafels'. I couldn't resist taking photos of
the huge array of fruit and vegetables of every colour and
description in the greengrocers; the trays of crusty rolls,
freshly baked and covered with sesame seeds, standing
beside the trays of pitta bread which we watched baking
in the glowing open ovens. Ezekiel had foretold this.

'*You will live in the land I gave your forefathers . . . I will
call for the grain and make it plentiful . . . I will increase the
fruit of the trees and the crops of the field. . . .*'

(Ezekiel 36: 28–30)

180

Isaiah prophesied that foreigners would help to rebuild Israel. Here were the photos of the lovely buildings, surrounded by fertile gardens and orchards which were cared for by four German Lutheran brothers, who daily prayed for Israel and the Jewish people, as well as for Church unity.

'Foreigners will rebuild your walls . . . .'

(Isaiah 60: 10)

We had visited a moshav near Jerusalem which was founded by Finnish Bible believers in 1971. In their brochure it stated that 'they wished to settle among the Jews, and help them rebuild the land'. I remembered a young Swedish man at our kibbutz, who had come to work with the Jewish people.

'Aliens will shepherd your flocks; foreigners will work your fields and vineyards.'

(Isaiah 61: 5)

I had three photographs of a huge, dark, bronze sculpture, the 'Scrolls of Fire'. It was 27 feet high and was situated in the Judean hills. It showed the history of the Jewish nation, from their persecution in the Holocaust, till they finally entered their promised land.

My German room mate, Margret, who had been a small child during the holocaust, wept bitterly as we prayed by this memorial sculpture. John, a young Anglican vicar, cried out in repentance for the actions of the British to the Jewish people after the war.

Again – I had witnessed the fulfillment of prophecy.

'The sons (and daughters) *of your oppressors will come bowing before you; all who despise you will bow down at your feet. . . .'*

(Isaiah 60: 14)

181

We were sons and daughters of those who had oppressed the Jewish people, and here we were, bowing in repentance.

How extraordinary. I had no knowledge of any of this when I went to Israel, yet God had clearly guided me, even in my photography. Through them I was shown that the words of the prophets were being fulfilled.

Another prophecy in Isaiah astonished me.

'Who are these that fly along like clouds, like doves to their nests? . . . . in the lead are the ships of Tarshish, bringing your sons from afar with their silver and gold . . . .'

(Isaiah 60: 8–9)

How could Isaiah have known that every day, at Tel Aviv airport, thousands of Jewish people would return by aeroplane, from Russia, Ethiopia, etc. Isaiah's clouds, or doves flying along, would be the aeroplanes that he would never see.

I realised as I read the prophets that over and over again, the return of the Jewish people to Israel had been foretold.

'The days are coming,' declares the Lord, 'when I will bring my people Israel and Judah back from captivity and restore them to the land I gave to their forefathers to possess; says the Lord.'

(Jeremiah 30: 3)

'. . . . I will gather you from the nations and bring you back from the countries where you have been scattered, and I will give you back the land of Israel again.'

(Ezekiel 11: 17)

It was also prophesied that when this occurs, the Jewish people will know spiritual renewal.

'But now listen, O Jacob, my servant, Israel, whom I have chosen. This is what the Lord says . . . "I will pour

out my Spirit on your offspring, and my blessing on your descendants".'

(Isaiah 44: 1–3)

'And I will pour out on the house of David and the inhabitants of Jerusalem a spirit of grace and supplication.'
(Zechariah 12: 10)

I puzzled over Romans 11. I had never really understood what the 'olive tree' was. But now I realised – I was grafted onto Jewish roots. No wonder I felt such a love for the Jewish people; I was part of them. How could I or the Church survive without roots?

But what was this olive tree? I asked a few people who knew the Bible well, but didn't get a satisfactory answer until I asked Tony Morton.

'It's the Kingdom of God,' he said.

Well praise God, of course! God's chosen people – the Jewish nation, as the root of the olive tree – had been selected and prepared for the coming of Jesus to earth.

But they had been crushed and cut off (as Jesus was), so that we, the Gentiles, could be grafted in. But now that the times of the Gentiles is coming to fulfilment, Jesus will be revealed to the Jewish nation, and the natural branches, (the Jews), will rapidly be grafted back, to grow together beside the unnatural branches.

'So too, at the present time there is a remnant (of the Jewish people) *chosen by grace . . . . because of their transgression, salvation has come to the Gentiles . . . . and their loss means riches for the Gentiles, how much greater riches will their fulness bring . . . . if the root* (the Jewish people) *is holy, so are the branches . . . . you, though a wild olive shoot, have been grafted in . . . and now share in the nourishing sap from the olive root . . . You do not support the root, but the root supports you . . . if they* (the Jewish people) *do not persist in unbelief, they will be grafted in, for God is able to graft them in again. After all, if you were cut out of an olive*

183

tree that is wild by nature, and contrary to nature were grafted into a cultivated olive tree, how much more readily will these, the natural branches, be grafted into their own olive tree?'

(Romans 11: 5, 11, 12, 16–18, 23–24)

How great indeed will be our riches when God grafts back the Jewish branches. How grateful we should be for the nourishing sap we receive from our Holy Jewish roots, which counteract the effects of the polluted sap of our pagan ancestry.

I started to think about the dispersal (diaspora) of the Jews all over the world. Was it because the root (the Jewish nation) was broken up that the Church was divided?

I realised that as the Jewish people have returned to Israel, so the Church has started to move towards unity. It was in 1948 that the Jewish nation was re-established in Israel. Was it just a coincidence that in the same year the World Council of Churches was formed in Amsterdam?

I could see a parallel process taking place, one strand being the homecoming and renewal of the Jewish nation to Israel, the other, the gathering in of the Gentiles, and the uniting of the Church.

What is happening to the Jewish nation is important for Church unity. Why? Because the Jewish nation is the root of the olive tree (the Kingdom of God on earth). As that root has been torn and uprooted, and planted out in many countries, so the Gentile branches, grafted onto this root, have reflected that brokenness in the divided Church. Now that Israel, the root, is becoming whole again (as the Jewish people return to Israel, and are replanted in their own land) so the ingrafted branches, the Gentile Christians, can also become whole and united. Allelluia!

But were these just my thoughts taking a ramble, or was God speaking to me?

'Please Father confirm this to me if it is from You,' I cried. I looked up from my typewriter towards the garden. The sky was dark with storm clouds, then, a brilliant rainbow appeared, and, as I watched, two doves flew side by side across the rainbow. One dove was pure white, the other one was a mixture of grey, black and white.

Yes, it was from God, the pure white dove representing the Jewish believer in Jesus, who comes from a holy and pure genetic stock, equally shares the promises of God with the Gentile believer, represented by the mottled dove from a pagan background, that contains a mixture of good and evil influences.

It didn't matter. God's promises through Jesus were equally shared by Messianic Jew and Gentile believer. We were brothers and sisters in the new covenant.

The Church needs to accept its Jewish roots, so that the Jew being grafted back onto the olive tree can become one with the Gentile believers. This will bring unity, joy and fulfilment to the whole Church, and will herald the return of Jesus.

Amen and Amen. Come Lord Jesus, Come.

Let us rejoice with the angels at the coming fulfilment of God's plan for the Church and for Israel.

'Rejoice with Jerusalem and be glad for her, all you who love her; rejoice greatly with her. . . .'

(Isaiah 66: 10)

'Father, we repent of our lack of love and gratitude to our Jewish roots, and pray to be freed of any wrong attitudes in our hearts for the Jews. Father, forgive us, we have not understood. Please heal the Jewish people from the hurts, pain and fear they have received in the past. Pour out Your Spirit on them that they may find Jesus as their Messiah, so that the natural branches can be grafted back.

Father, complete the gathering in of the Gentiles, so that the olive tree will be whole and complete and the Kingdom of God will be established on earth as it is in Heaven.'

'. . . . the Kingdom of the world has become the kingdom of our Lord and of his Christ, and he will reign for ever and ever.'

(Revelation 11: 15)

'Amen! Praise and glory and wisdom and thanks and honour and power and strength be to our God for ever and ever. Amen!'

(Revelation 7: 12)

Epilogue:

A Cry from the Heart

Whilst reading 'Love Covers' by Paul Bilheimer, the arguments for and against charismatics and non-charismatics suddenly exploded around me.

I wept for the Church, crying out to God for His mercy, then I wrote the following:

I do not understand theologians who sit in judgment on charismatics, or charismatics who dismiss non-charismatics.

We are all nothing beside the broken body of Christ. Our sins are like scarlet, but He through His supreme sacrifice, has made them as white as snow. (Isaiah 1: 18)

Nothing that we have done or said makes us acceptable to God. It is not our denominational label, Church of England, Roman Catholic, Baptist, Methodist, Pentecostal, House Church etc. that will save us, only that we have received and acknowledged the shed blood of Jesus as the cover for our sinfulness.

Even today I have discovered Christians who think that anyone who prays for the Jewish people, or for the nation of Israel, believing that the promises of the prophets are for them, must be a misguided fanatic!

But these praying Christians have heard from God, and are obeying His leading. If that is His will for them, who are we to judge and try to prove that they are wrong?

God has made us as different parts of a body,

'The eye cannot say to the hand, "I don't need you!" And the head cannot say to the feet, "I don't need you!"'

(1 Corinthians 12: 21)

No, all parts of the body are needed, but for different purposes. God cannot be contained in one person's mind, we are each given some part of the truth. That is why we need to listen to each other with humility. Jesus said,

'Do not judge, or you too will be judged. For in the same way you judge others, you will be judged . . . .'

(Matthew 7: 1)

The spiritual Israel is indeed the new nation out of all nations, that truly serves Christ. But Israel is also a geographic location, where, in earthly terms, God is showing us the progress of the spiritual through a physical outworking of prophecy!

God is Spirit, yet Jesus came to earth as a man, to show us the spiritual truth of God in His earthly life and death.

God is using the same method today to guide, help and encourage us. Let us not miss what He is telling us through the Jewish people and Israel, or we will be guilty of the same sin as theirs, when they rejected Jesus. Jesus was also a physical presence sent to show us in real terms God's plan for the world.

We need to acknowledge our lack of love and understanding, and our bias as we try to mould Scripture to fit our own ideas and theories.

'He (**Jesus**) said to them, "Let the little children come to me . . . . for the kingdom of God belongs to such, as these. I tell you the truth, anyone who will not receive the kingdom of God like a little child will never enter it."'

(Mark 10: 14–15)

Little children wouldn't write proofs that one group of Christians is more enlightened, more godly and more correct theologically than another. They would listen to their Father, and acknowledge that they know very little, and have a lot to learn, and, even then, will never know all the answers. They would not lecture their Father on who is right, and who is wrong, for surely this is what we do. God forgive us. No one is right except God, '. . . . *and all our righteous acts are like filthy rags.* . . .' (Isaiah 64: 6).

May we come to God on our knees like little children, knowing nothing, and pray to God with humility to reveal the truth to us, or the tiny fraction that our minds can cope with.

'*Oh, the depth of the riches of the wisdom and knowledge of God! How unsearchable his judgments, and his paths beyond tracing out! Who has known the mind of the Lord? Or who has been his counsellor?*'

(Romans 11: 33–34)

We think our ideas and thoughts are so important. But what is important beside the broken body of Christ?

Have we lost our hearts? Where are they? Are they imprisoned in the pride of our minds?

'. . . . *We are the clay, you are the potter, we are all the work of your hand.*'

(Isaiah 64: 8)

Shall the pot argue with the potter and tell Him that He should make all His pots the same?

Jesus, forgive us, forgive us. We have forgotten how to weep, how to put on sackcloth and ashes, to fast and mourn for Your broken Church, Your broken world, for the lost, the hungry, the unloved.

We have forgotten that You do not recommend those who have all the answers, and know the right way to be a Christian, and who have the best knowledge and understanding of Your word. You only recommend those

who follow the way of love, loving their neighbour as
themselves, laying down their lives for each other, giving
their time, their money, their possessions, their love to
those in need.

'. . . . *I tell you the truth, whatever you did for one of the
least of these brothers of mine, you did for me.*'

(Matthew 25: 40)

Oh Jesus, that we could all come together in our
nakedness to the foot of the cross, pleading and weeping
for mercy on our knees, repenting of our divisions, and
begging for them to be healed.

Forgive us the pain and hurt our divisions cause You.
May we die to our pride and self-righteousness, and
embrace with love our Christian brothers and sisters,
accepting them as You have accepted us, unconditionally,
with tenderness and joy, sharing their pains and hurts.

May we not pass by on the other side (Luke 10: 31)
leaving Your broken Body, and Your suffering world to
die.

Could you look on His agony
Could you?
Could you?
Could you look on His agony,
and not die too?

We all look,
We all pass by,
We leave Him
to die.

'May this not be true of us Jesus. May we stop, and
pour in the healing oil of Your love. To bind up the
wounds, that your Body, the Church, may be whole
again'. Amen.

Jesus prayed, '. . . . *May they be brought to complete unity to let the world know that you sent me and have loved them even as you have loved me.*'

(John 17: 23)

'Thank you Jesus; We know that Your prayer for us will be answered.'

Bibliography

Father Make Us One – Floyd McClung
The Meeting of the Waters – George Carey
Love Covers – Paul Bilheimer
Divided We Stand – Gerald Coates
How to Spot a Church Split – Donald Bridge
In the Crucible – Robert Warren
The Radical Christian – Arthur Wallis
Priest in Prison – John Hayter
Saint Francis of Assissi – John R. H. Moorman
Nine-o'clock in the Morning – Dennis Bennett
The Adversary – Mark Bubeck
Defeated Enemies – Corrie Ten Boom
Spiritual Warfare – Derek Prince
Spiritual Warfare – Michael Harper
Intercession – Andrew Murray
Intercessory Prayer – Leonard E LeSourd
Tears of Intercession – June Coxhead
Prayer, Key to Revival – Paul Y Cho
Battle Stations – Peter Gammons
Territorial Spirits – C Peter Wagner
The Unseen World of Angels and Demons – Basilea Schlink
Demons Defeated – Bill Subritzky
God's Powerful Weapon – Dennis Lane
Healing through Deliverance – Peter Horrobin
Free to Live – Liesl Alexander
Explaining Spiritual Protection – Lance Lambert
A Sound of Joy – David and Dale Garrett
Winning the Prayer War – Kjell Sjöberg
Join Our Hearts – Stephen Abbot
Build That Bridge – David Coffey
The Church in Ruins – Dr. William Crabb and Jeff Jernigan